Copyright © 2017 by Schiffer Publishing, Ltd.

Originally published as *Survival Guide für Echte Kerle* by Verlag pietsch © 2015 Paul-Pietsch Verlag
Translated from the German by Omicron Language Solutions, LLC

Library of Congress Control Number: 2017935608

Cover design by John Cheek
Type set in Boycott/Impact/BentonSans
Layout concept by Patricia Braun / www.patriciabraun.de
All images by Joe Vogel and Patricia Braun

ISBN: 978-0-7643-5426-7
Printed in China

Published by Schiffer Publishing, Ltd.
4880 Lower Valley Road
Atglen, PA 19310
Phone: (610) 593-1777; Fax: (610) 593-2002
E-mail: Info@schifferbooks.com
Web: www.schifferbooks.com

For our complete selection of fine books on this and related subjects, please visit our website at www.schifferbooks.com. You may also write for a free catalog.

Schiffer Publishing's titles are available at special discounts for bulk purchases for sales promotions or premiums. Special editions, including personalized covers, corporate imprints, and excerpts, can be created in large quantities for special needs. For more information, contact the publisher.

We are always looking for people to write books on new and related subjects. If you have an idea for a book, please contact us at proposals@schifferbooks.com.

Note: *The killing of wild animals is strictly regulated by law. You can practice methods for hunting and trapping without animals, though these may only be used on animals in a legitimate emergency. You should care for and protect all types of life that you do not need either to live on or for training. Always remain aware of the responsibility entrusted to you by the knowledge described herein.*

LEGEND

AT A GLANCE

Here you will find the essential knowledge and basic techniques required for every important survival situation coded by letter and number. This way you are sure to be able to meet any challenge.

FIRE

WATER

SHELTER

RATIONS

MEDICINE

EQUIPMENT

KNOW-HOW/SKILLS

THEMES TRANSCENDING THE CHAPTERS

 KNOTS

 NAVIGATION

CONTENTS

There may be people who regard survival—the art of living and surviving independently outdoors—as an anachronism. Water just comes from the water main, power from the wall outlet, and supermarket shelves are always full. Even during a serious event—a flood, power outage, or blizzard—we are in a good situation. Emergency services, fire departments, and not least, huge grocery stores are very good at keeping people safe.

But things look very different when we leave our home territory to go backpacking in Siberia, take a safari in Africa, or a fishing trip on the remote rivers of Australia. In such places—"in the wilderness"—if you lose your equipment, your car breaks down, or your rental boat capsizes it can quickly have consequences, and you may find yourself in a survival situation.

This is where this book comes in.

Survival training in your local woods is an exciting, fulfilling, and challenging task: while you spend a relaxing end of the day by athletically drilling a fire, barbecuing, carving, or collecting edible wild plants you are preparing yourself for an emergency when the tools and resources you need are not available.

Knowledge of food, bait, knots, and plants will **always** give you an advantage, whether you are a hiker, geocacher, mountain climber, angler, or just an individual or "normal" vacationer. Your ability to do what is necessary with your bare hands, minimal equipment, and experience gives you self-confidence and opens up new paths when choosing travel destinations.

The first time you retire to your makeshift shelter in the jungle or in the forest after a dinner you gathered yourself, listening to the animals in the forest and gazing at the night sky, you will understand this only works **with nature** and not "versus the wild."

It would be an unequal fight.

For your **work with nature**, which may be a new challenge for you, I wish you much success.

Yours, Joe Vogel

You are going to find a vast range of survival techniques and instructions for many different situations in books and on the Internet. I want to keep things a bit more clear here. Practicing realistic techniques with minimal equipment lets you improvise a great deal in an emergency without instructions. You will find the most important basics for starting out in the next chapter.

SURVIVAL BASICS

BASICS: EQUIPMENT

The question of what is appropriate survival equipment is a classic paradox. "Survival" is an attempt (in an emergency, a compulsion) to survive using minimal equipment in a situation where you have unexpectedly gotten into a struggle for survival or lost your baggage.

But it would be presumptuous to assume that a beginner would be able to survive outside "with nothing at all." Therefore, in this section we present the most important equipment—along with a statement of understanding that in the course of training, you will gradually learn to do without it, and only take it along as a backup. Instead of using a tent and sleeping bag, soon you will be building a shelter. You can do without a lighter and a knife once you have learned how to cut things with stones and make a fire using a drill; with each training session you will cut back on your supplies, be able to gather edible wild plants, and hunt animals.

Equipment for survival training differs from ordinary camping or hiking equipment since it must be sturdier and withstand sparks.

Here I present survival packs and equipment that can be used while training.

E1 THE RIGHT KNIFE

If you ask ten people about the right knife you will get ten different answers.

Is there really any right knife?

In my opinion yes, but not in the sense of those described as the "right knife" in some outdoor forums and articles. The best knife is the one which you have at hand in an emergency and during training, whether it is a broken-off kitchen knife, a jackknife, or a flint blade.

It is not the polished piece in a glass case too valuable to be used, but the one you trained with and which is appropriate for your hand size and experience. People usually select survival knives that are too big. You can make and build anything using a good machete that you can also do with a small knife, but you are more likely to have a small knife with you in an emergency. Above all, you need much more practice when working with a large blade than with a small knife. It does not help much if you can split wood using a powerful combat knife but cannot make a fire drill, since the latter requires very precise carving.

You might want to get yourself a "portable" knife and practice with it regularly.

Blade shape, cut, and so on are a matter of taste. Then there are some "innovations" in recent years which are of little use: a serrated blade has no practical advantage and often interferes with your work, and "wilderness survival knives" nearly a centimeter thick are neither appropriate for chopping nor for cutting.

A classic knife with a rounded handle and a blade that is not too long, but very sharp, is still the best choice for most techniques. They have been used for centuries by practitioners worldwide.

I personally value the following features:

An opening for attaching a lanyard.

Near the handle the back of the knife should be fluted for a safe thumb rest.

A round, smooth handle with grooves allows you to use it safely without getting tired.

The lower third of the knife has a sharp edge for rubbing a fire steel and for peeling roots.

A simple polish and a sharpening notch make sharpening easier in the field.

Fine quality: An old fire starter knife with saw, striking edge, and a useful blade.

Always there: Anyone experienced with small knives can always carry one along. They are light and hardly bother you.

A typical beginner's knife: A strong blade that can be well sharpened. The handle and sheath are made of easy-to-clean materials.

Pretty, functional, but not quite safe: It should be possible to secure open blades.

A simple vine cutting knife: With a carbon blade that can be secured.

Can do everything, but nothing right: Such tool batteries fit your hand badly and weigh a lot.

11

E2 ASSEMBLING THE OPTIMAL SURVIVAL KIT

The survival kit is the equipment you must always have about you when you are on a trip. If you lose your equipment you still have your survival kit.

The general rule: The more experienced you are the smaller the survival kit can be—the smaller the survival kit, the more likely you will have it along in an emergency.

If you have to carry a full backpack to ignite a fire, to build a makeshift shelter, and to treat water, as well as take along emergency rations to eat, it is more likely you will lose that than you would lose a micro survival kit on a key chain or a small knife. **The more survival you have in your mind the less kit you need on your person.**

Commercial survival kits should be adapted based on your own knowledge and experience and expanded or cut back. Important in general: The survival kit is also your practice device. Anyone who only opens their survival container for the first time in an emergency has the cards stacked against them!

CHECKLIST
WHAT BELONGS IN A SURVIVAL KIT?

- ☐ To make a fire: Fire steel or lighter, or matches
- ☐ A sharp knife
- ☐ Fishing line with hooks
- ☐ Rescue blanket
- ☐ Signal whistle
- ☐ Signal mirror
- ☐ Compass
- ☐ Condom (always a lifesaver)
- ☐ Wire
- ☐ Sturdy cord
- ☐ Needles
- ☐ Scalpel or razor blade
- ☐ Smoke cartridges
- ☐ Water purification tablets
- ☐ Money
- ☐ Bandage material
- ☐ Flashlight or headlamp

SURVIVAL CONTAINER Anyone who likes to keep things simple can also fall back on ready-made survival containers or survival kits. Due to their weight it only makes sense to carry such containers in a backpack, or you can store them in your vehicle in case of an accident, breakdown, etc. Especially for longer trips, you should equip and expand your survival kit with professional tools. Make sure the material is high-quality, and replace anything worn out after you have practiced with it.

SURVIVAL POUCH Pack your most important tools and some money in a sealable, waterproof bag: paracord, whistle, push button compass, condom, flint, knife, a small lamp, and so on. The bag should not be too heavy, so you can still easily carry it hanging or in a trouser pocket. You should also be sure, for space reasons, to only pack one each of reusable tools: one lighter, one knife, etc.

MINI SURVIVAL KIT Small, waterproof capsules which can be attached to a key ring make an ideal survival kit, especially for long distance travel, when all your equipment can be lost or stolen; this is your safeguard for getting back home in healthy condition. It should include the following: a micro SD card with all your travel documents (birth certificate, etc.) filed down on the sides to make it fit; at least $100 or the equivalent in local currency; a universal lighter for starting fires; fishhooks to catch small fish, birds, etc.; a scalpel as a tool for cutting cords and making tools and traps; and water purification tablets.

MICRO SURVIVAL KIT The smallest survival kit of all consists of just your knowledge and your hands. **There are some who even say "anything more than a knife is camping."** Since you usually have a knife with you outdoors anyway you can consider it "standard kit." If you still need a lighter for lighting fires you have to practice more.

Survival container:
You should practice using the contents of commercially packed survival kits before any emergency happens and adapt the contents to your needs.

▶

SURVIVAL KIT
DIE 15 WICHTIGSTEN
TOOLS IM FILER BOX

DMAX

Survival pouch:
Small enough and contains everything you need.

◀

DMAX
© 2013 DCL

Mini survival kit:
Only for pros—you can do anything with this kit if you have practiced enough.

▶

E3 GADGETS IN DETAIL

A small selection of items that will make your life in the outdoors easier and are a big help for training:

Lamp: Helps you set up camp or catching animals after dark.

Slingshot: For hunting small animals.

Compass: Always shows you the way. Definitely in combination with a good hiking map!

ÜBERLEBENSRATION
(2 Rationssätze)
Kohlenhydratkomprimat

Versorgungsnummer: 8970-12-313-1932
Verpflegungsration, Überleben

Hergestellt: 2014

200g

Signal flares: To make your location noticeable in an emergency.

Survival rations: Keep you fit until you have gathered enough food.

Condoms and a scalpel: Equipment for your wallet.

Rescue blanket: The thin reflecting foil protects you from getting chilled.

Poncho: A lightweight raincoat you should always pack, even in good weather.

Bivouac tent: If a rainstorm has destroyed your hut of greenery during the night.

E4 SHELTER TO GO

Constructing a shelter is particularly time consuming during survival training and when on a trip. This work may take several hours to complete due to the time it takes to collect building materials—wood, leaves, brush wood, and so on.

If you want to build your own shelter anew every night during training or when on a challenging hike, you lose a lot of time for doing other important things. Of course, you should still know how to improvise a shelter (→ **debris hut**) and also practice this regularly. All the same, in the beginning you should always carry a light type of shelter adapted to the area, such as a tent, tarp, or bivouac tent, together with a suitable sleeping bag.

TARP How useful carrying a tarp is depends on the environment and weather conditions: in the desert and Outback tarps can provide shade, while in the forest, rainforest, and at a barbecue they can be used as a rain shelter. You can also improvise one using a rescue blanket or poncho. They are less suitable in the mountains, at very low temperatures, and in storms.

SLEEPING BAG Sleeping bags come in various sizes and degrees of warmth. What counts here is that down is certainly significantly warmer than a comparable amount of synthetic fiber (hollow fiber and the like), but it clumps together when wet, so in the tropics and during exercises in muddy conditions synthetic fiber is the better choice. In the desert, snow, and ice, and in the mountains people usually use down sleeping bags.

CAMPING MAT When sleeping on the ground you can lose a lot of heat if the place where you are lying is not insulated. Here it makes absolute sense to make a → **field mattress** or carry along a camping mat.

Self-inflating mats or air mattresses: Comfortable, but heavy and easily damaged.
▶

Foam camping mat: Indestructible, but therefore offers a bit less comfort.
◀

Sleeping bag: A warming layer of insulation which should be cut wide enough.
▶

Tarp: rain cover and sun canopy in one.
▼

E5 MY TENT IS MY CASTLE

For the entire time you are out hiking, your tent will be your most secure shelter. It makes no sense to save on this important piece of equipment. A tent usually consists of an outer and inner tent; only very light tents and → **bivy sacks** have one layer. Since tents are waterproof they should always be well ventilated, otherwise the walls drip condensation.

Which tent you choose depends on where you are traveling. In the mountains, it is good to use a light but storm-proof geodesic tent with an inner tent that can be closed tightly and a lot of guy ropes and closeable vents; when traveling through deserts and on the steppes an inner mosquito tent with a rain-proof cover is often used; and in snowy regions, a spacious tunnel tent with a vestibule big enough to accommodate snowshoes, a sled, and backpacks. The outer tent is often made of PU-coated fabric; high-quality tents are also made of siliconized nylon. Frames are now mostly made of aluminum and are only rarely fiberglass.

Inexpensive dome tents are still good enough for a rainy weekend at a rock festival, but if you take such a tent into the wilderness, you should be well practiced building a → **shelter**.

E6 BACKPACKS AND BAGS

If you are out on the road, what you take along depends on your level of training and the travel region, from a shelter as backup to a sleeping bag for freezing temperatures. But you do not always need a big backpack. Often just a simple, good belt bag or small carrying system will suffice. It is ideal if you can carry everything you need in your clothing.

▶ *Backpack:* For all your hiking equipment.

Carrying system: Here you will find enough space for your training survival materials. ◀

Sled: A pulka is a real advantage in snow and ice. ▼

E7 SHOES, BOOTS, AND SOCKS

One piece of equipment that you always have along—whether on a survival tour or a hiking trip—is boots or hiking shoes.

There are various styles made and distributed by dozens of manufacturers. Here we will outline the most important basic styles.

Almost as important as the right foot gear is an extra pair of good socks.

Modern hiking socks: Are light, dry quickly, and snuggle up well on your foot. These are particularly suitable for moderate temperatures.
▶

Neoprene socks: If you cannot determine whether your trip will end in wet mud you should pack a pair of waterproof socks. These are also available with a breathable "biomembrane." They turn your street shoes into rubber boots.
▶

Sheep's wool socks: These never become old—it is hard to beat well-knitted sheep's wool socks for warmth, comfort, and foot climate. They are the right choice when it will be colder.
▶

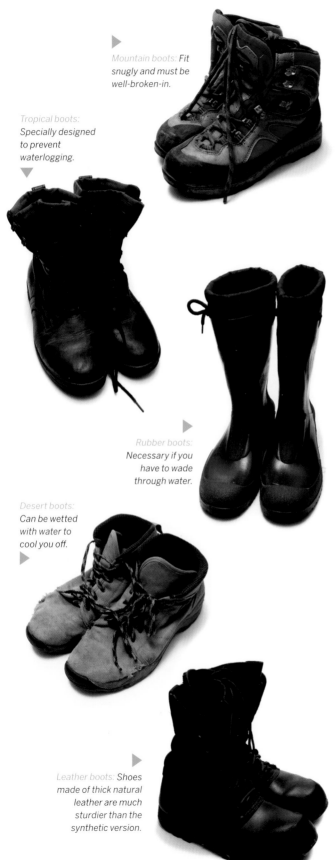

Mountain boots: Fit snugly and must be well-broken-in.

Tropical boots: Specially designed to prevent waterlogging.

Rubber boots: Necessary if you have to wade through water.

Desert boots: Can be wetted with water to cool you off.

Leather boots: Shoes made of thick natural leather are much sturdier than the synthetic version.

MOUNTAIN BOOTS can be laced tightly and must fit your feet well. Besides providing protection from stones and the possibility of attaching crampons, the rigid sole is a typical feature. Alpine shoes are unbeatable in the mountains; on plateaus there are often more comfortable alternatives.

TROPICAL BOOTS In regions where there are poisonous and biting animals, boots which go above the ankles are always practical. Tropical boots also have a sewn-on tongue (against blood-flukes), very slip-resistant soles, and are water repellent, but also often have a "drain opening" where water that has seeped in can drain out.

RUBBER BOOTS In wet regions and when hiking in water rubber boots are often worn. They are completely waterproof, and with socks can even be worn in colder temperatures. When worn this way there is no problem walking a long way in them. In the evening you should air and dry them.

DESERT BOOTS In the desert, you often sink in when walking in soft sand. If sand gets into your shoes you will get blisters and chafing. Unlike tropical boots, desert boots are usually made of a lightweight cotton fabric which absorbs moisture and lets the feet cool by evaporation.

BOOTS FOR THE FOREST High and very sturdy leather boots are classic and can prevent twisting and slipping, and therefore injury, in wooded areas. Especially when you are working with a hatchet or ax these boots offer a (certain) additional protection if it should slip.

E8 WATER FILTERS AND PURIFICATION TABLETS

When you are underway you always have to supply yourself with water. If things go wrong, it may be the only thing you can find is a dirty pond. There are safe, improvised treatment methods, but if you want cover a few miles during the day tools to sterilize water are a great advantage.

Simple water filter: Turns every puddle into drinkable water.

◀

Water purification tablets (such as Micropur Forte): Should be in every survival kit. They can sterilize small amounts of water safely.

E9 FIRE STARTER — LET IT BURN!

Simple lighters are always helpful as a backup. What counts here is, with anything that uses gas or gasoline, there is always a danger it will not work: gas from gas lighters can leak when the lever is pressed; the flint may wear out; and piezo igniters do not work when damp. Gasoline often evaporates from a normal storm lighter in a few days. In contrast, the following are useful survival lighters:

Waterproof packed matches: Matches are still the classic for starting a fire. You should carry a few storm matches and a few with a normal igniting head in a waterproof box.

▼

Firesteel: Always works—even if you have fallen in water and everything is soaked. But you have to practice how to carve the finest tinder from wood to ignite a flame or carry along a cotton pad with wax.

▼

Magnesium starter: Always provides tinder. Magnesium is scraped from the block as tinder and ignited with the inset spark rod. Burns extremely hot and reliably ignites fine wood.

▶

E10 COOKING ON YOUR TRIP

For heating water and preparing food in extreme situations and in areas where there is little or no natural fuel stoves are very useful devices. Even if your aim is to cook over the fire, a small "backup device" in your backpack is a valuable aid when you cannot light a cooking fire in the pouring rain.

We divide these roughly into gas, gasoline, and wood stoves.

WOOD STOVES (HOBO OVEN)

are heated with natural fuels. These metal boxes are handy mobile fireplaces. The design creates a chimney effect—heat is emitted effectively. As a result, the fuel burns much more efficiently than in a campfire. Suitable especially for regions where there is little firewood, or where an open fire on the ground can cause a → **bush fire**.

GAS STOVES

are fueled with a gas mixture which can be bought in a screw- or twist-on cartridge. They burn quietly, efficiently, and cleanly. Depending on the region you might not be able to find suitable cartridges, so a puncture cartridge adapter is useful. Gas stoves are used mainly in the mountains.

MULTI-FUEL STOVES

burn with all petroleum-based fuels, such as diesel, kerosene, gasoline, or lamp oil. Especially when traveling in snowy regions and deserts these stoves are a great help, since the fuel required burns very economically and is easy to get anywhere, and is often carried in your vehicle anyway.

Wood stove:
You can cook using a hobo stove when there is little fuel available.

Gas stove:
Burns cleanly and odor free. A gas stove is especially useful in the mountains.

Multi-fuel stove:
Works cost-effectively, and fuel is obtainable all over the world: gasoline, diesel, and lamp oil.

You have to practice everything you do outdoors, from simple backpacking to starting a fire with a match. The less equipment you have available, the more important your skills for finding alternatives or making suitable tools.

In this section we will first deal with the basics. Special techniques and skills are divided among their respective fields of application, but that does not mean they cannot be applied elsewhere.

It is best to always keep a specific scenario in mind, collect the relevant instructions from the individual chapters, and practice these in a meaningful order.

This way, you can keep shrinking your survival kit until you can do absolutely everything, from lighting a fire to catching animals, with your bare hands.

Your engagement with survival should not mean your goal is to have the biggest possible survival kit in your backpack, but rather, a kit that is as complete as possible in your head.

W1 SEARCHING FOR SIGNS OF WATER — FINDING DRINKING WATER

In hilly terrain it is seldom hard to find water. In practice, you only have to hike downhill until you find, at the lowest point, or ultimately in the valley, a river, or at least damp earth.

In the hills, a saddle is a typical place to find water. These plateaus often form a basin. You can often find clear and small springs in particular types of hill structures.

Mountains have a shape like two slopes were pushed into each other. Usually emerging from a saddle, the slope first breaks steeply downward and runs down into the valley. You can generally find water on such a watershed in the mountain slope, since this structure forms the fastest way out of the slopes. Therefore, it is the lowest place respectively on the mountain where you will find water.

In warmer regions such open water bodies can be found by bird cries. Many animal trails also lead to water holes. Plant signs of water are reeds, pandanus, ferns and mosses, rushes, and water-loving trees like willow or poplar.

Steep valleys indicate torrential rivers can flow down them after storms. If you dig in the river bed you will find water long after it has rained.

Typical water pointers in North American and European latitudes: Ferns, moss, and horsetails only grow well in really damp soil.

W2 BOILING DRINKING WATER

One of the safest water treatment methods that works anywhere in the world is boiling water. It is often discussed whether it is sufficient to boil drinking water briefly or whether it has to boil for at least ten or thirty minutes, and how safe boiling water is at higher altitudes.

For this I note the following:

>> Normal drinking water is never sterile, and also does not have to be sterile. Drinking water is "disinfected," and thus free of pathogens.

>> There are lots of germs, or dormant forms of them, that survive a short boiling and a half-hour boiling. However, these do not often cause diseases.

>> Every 984 ft. (300 m.) of altitude reduces the boiling point of water by about 34°F (1°C).

>> Most of the pathogens that cause diseases in humans thrive at a temperature of about 98.6°F (37°C).

>> Germ-infested foods usually contain many times the potential pathogen concentration in raw water.

>> Worldwide many potentially highly infectious foods (milk, pork, natural casings, surface-fertilized vegetables, etc.) are consumed after brief heating.

>> The aim of safe food preparation is a core temperature of about 167–185°F (75°–85°C); milk (cryptosporidium, EHEC, etc.) is pasteurized at 167°F (75°C) for about thirty seconds.

>> A boiling temperature of 185°F (85°C) can still be reached at approximately 2.8 miles (4,500 m.) above sea level—at this height, almost anywhere in the world, you can collect clean snow or melt water.

>> Microscopically sized germs reach a core temperature of 185°F (85°C) after a split second of heating.

CONCLUSION: Boiling water for a short time—even if it is contaminated with germs—can always be considered a safe preparation method. Practically all living cells are destroyed just by being heated to 185°F (85°C). Otherwise robust unicellular parasites are especially sensitive to heat. Normal technical disinfection (not sterilization) for bottling is performed at 158°F (70°C).

Heat resistant bacteria and spores survive boiling for one hour.

Boiling water briefly is usually just fine, even if the source is dirty.
▼

R1 EDIBLE PLANTS WORLDWIDE

There are many millions of plants all over the world, very many of which are edible. If you are traveling in a foreign region and want to search for food, you have to actually know all the local plants to avoid poisoning. The frequently described "edibility test"* is not a safe way to find out whether a plant is edible. **Some dangerous deadly poisons only reach their full effect after several days.**

One way to stock up on edible plants worldwide is to collect the **"Dirty Dozen"**—a total of twelve plant species which are edible all over the world. You can find at least one of these species practically anywhere in the world. "Species" is the umbrella term for different types of plants (or varieties) that look much alike and are related to each other. For example, all the plants known as a rose or rose hip— whether an ornamental rose in the garden or a wild rose at the edge of the woods—are the same. The same applies to plantains or cattails.

With a bit of practice you will keep on finding these plants and be able to identify them easily—after reading this book you already know that they are edible. **It is important to know that some plants have to be specially prepared to make them digestible.**

To make an edibility test, after a smell test and skin contact, you first consume only a small amount of an unknown plant, and if you do not notice any symptoms of poisoning, a few hours later you eat larger and larger amounts.

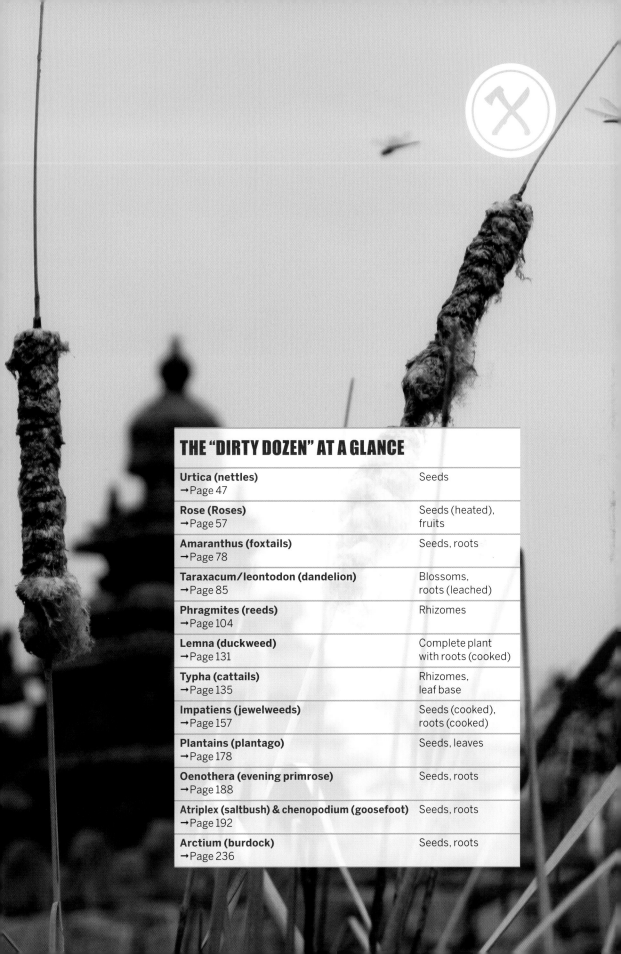

THE "DIRTY DOZEN" AT A GLANCE

Urtica (nettles) → Page 47	Seeds
Rose (Roses) → Page 57	Seeds (heated), fruits
Amaranthus (foxtails) → Page 78	Seeds, roots
Taraxacum/leontodon (dandelion) → Page 85	Blossoms, roots (leached)
Phragmites (reeds) → Page 104	Rhizomes
Lemna (duckweed) → Page 131	Complete plant with roots (cooked)
Typha (cattails) → Page 135	Rhizomes, leaf base
Impatiens (jewelweeds) → Page 157	Seeds (cooked), roots (cooked)
Plantains (plantago) → Page 178	Seeds, leaves
Oenothera (evening primrose) → Page 188	Seeds, roots
Atriplex (saltbush) & chenopodium (goosefoot) → Page 192	Seeds, roots
Arctium (burdock) → Page 236	Seeds, roots

R2 EATING INSECTS

If you are preparing insects, you should make sure you always remove all the wings, thin legs, and mandibles. These are made of chitin and do not provide any energy.

To kill insects, hold the head firmly with your thumb and index fingers, turn it 180°, and pull it gently away from the body. This also pulls the stomach out of the body.

Incidentally, it is perfectly normal if insects and other small animals still keep moving after being killed up to when they are cooked.

ATTENTION: For safety, all animal foods should be heated before consumption to kill any parasites.

R3 HUNTER'S EXPERT BUTCHERING

Use the same procedure to butcher all vertebrate animals: after stunning the animal open the blood vessels at the neck.

STUNNING Pick up mammals by the hind legs or by the tail; birds by the legs; and hold fish in your hand. Then use a wooden club to give several targeted and powerful blows to the back of the animal's head **(1)**. It should now be unconscious.

KILLING For mammals and birds, sever the neck up to the vertebrae **(2)**; for fish, slice the place where the gills merge into the side of the throat. After it is killed allow the animal to bleed for a few minutes.

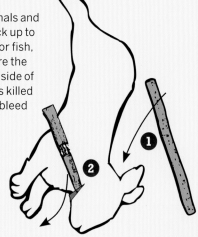

R4 GUTTING MAMMALS

If you have caught an animal you should gut it as quickly as possible, because after a few hours the internal organs begin to "digest themselves." The animal should be cut open as soon as possible after you have caught it or killed it in a trap. You can leave a little more time for → **skinning** off the hide.

It is important when dressing an animal not to let any of the bowel contents get into the abdominal cavity. If this happens the animal will only keep a much shorter time and must be quickly washed and cooked. It is best to hang large animals head down. You can also lay an animal down in front of you to dress it.

STEP 1 Cut the skin away from the lower jaw end to the rib cage. This exposes the gullet and windpipe.

STEP 2 Now carefully separate the abdomen from the breastbone to the hips. Here you must not cut into the intestines! When you have reached the hip bone, you cut the hide around the genitals and anus so it can be separated from the rest of the hide.

STEP 3 Then carefully separate the hip bones with the knife (for large animals you can also use a saw or a small ax) and fold the hip to the side.

STEP 4 Now reach into the abdominal cavity, hold the stomach tightly, and either pull the gullet through the rib cage or cut the gullet away from the abdominal cavity and cut through it. Pull the stomach out of the abdominal cavity and with it the bowel segments. The intestine is lifted from the spread-out hip bone and thus removed from the animal with the cut-free piece of skin so that the anus does not slip into the body.

STEP 5 Then remove all other organs (take care if the bladder is full) from the animal.

Before you use the animal, examine the liver (A), kidneys (you have to cut it lengthwise and "peel" off some membrane), and the spleen (B). The organs should have a solid color, be smooth and shiny, and not swollen. You can recognize the latter from the edges. If they are sharp-edged and not arched or bloated that is a good sign.

All the organs can be consumed except the stomach, intestines, testicles, and glands from the hip area, which sometimes have a strong taste. Many animals also have glands around the anus that should be cut away very carefully or everything will taste like a tiger cage.

After you gut a larger animal spread the abdominal cavity open. Pack everything up so it is protected from flies and hang it up for an hour to cool. If unrefrigerated, the animal should be processed or preserved by one to two days later.

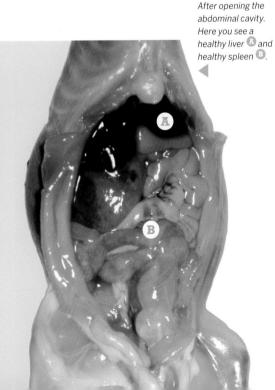

After opening the abdominal cavity. Here you see a healthy liver **A** *and healthy spleen* **B**.

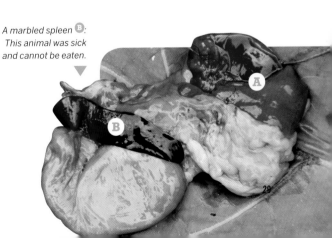

A marbled spleen **B**: *This animal was sick and cannot be eaten.*

On Life and Death

As the animal lies in front of me it is warm. I pick it up and feel the slight vibrations in its muscles which bear witness that death has occurred.

As a hunter who hunts and kills larger game, along with small mammals and reptiles, I do not feel euphoric joy or satisfaction over a successful hunt. Even if it took a lot of time and effort and when it assures my survival.

It is a life I have taken to feed myself. With appropriate respect I take care of the slain animal. It will take some time before the animal is plucked or skinned and gutted until it is clear it was healthy and can be cooked on the embers.

Killing a living being seems to be taboo today. Yet animals are constantly being killed—so casually that it is possible to ignore this. Each pre-packaged sausage was once part of a turkey or pig. You can buy half an animal life with french fries and ketchup at a fast food restaurant for a few dollars. Even a fish, cut up into rectangles and breaded, at best had a free life.

While many people want to eat meat, hardly anyone will take the responsibility upon themselves to kill an animal with their own hands, to sense the flow of warm blood through their hands and smell the organs as you dress the meat.

So many criticize hunting to me, the deliberate killing and use of an animal, but I am sure that this way of obtaining food on a journey or in an emergency is justified, as well as gathering plants, in that human beings often can only survive in such a situation if we put ourselves on a level with animals that end the lives of other animals to eat.

K1 COLD SMOKING MEAT AND FISH

With a process very like → **smoke tanning** you can also preserve your own ham or fish. You can make a cold smoker from a stack of stones or logs which is ventilated well enough so that wind can cool the interior of the smoker. You should cover the upper part with large leaves or bark so that smoke builds up in the smoker. To smoke something, put strongly smoldering logs in the oven and replace them regularly.

Cold smoking works best as a way of preserving pieces that have been cut into strips. Cold smoking takes from a few hours up to several days, depending on the thickness of the smoked food. For thin strips which dry at the same time, three to four hours is sufficient.

After smoking they are dried and left to "draw." Smoked and dried products keep for many weeks.

◄

A smoker can be built quickly, but the cold smoking process may take several days.

M1 AN EMERGENCY BANDAGE

Whatever natural fiber you use, it must be parched.

▼

When outdoors you often cut, scrape, or tear open your skin, so you should always have a few small bandages to keep wounds clean. You can also make your own bandages, but that is not so simple, because the surface which contacts the wound should be sterile, or at least should not be contaminated with germs. **Simple boiling is not sufficient to sterilize materials.** But you can immerse a rag or piece of clothing in a concentrated solution of water purification tablets (one tablet for about a shot glass of water) or "iron" it on a heated stone. You can also sterilize natural fibers such as tree fungi this way. Damp materials cannot be sterilized with dry heat, however, because they are heated by the water they contain to a maximum of 212°F (100°C) —too low to kill all germs dangerous for open wounds.

What you should not do: Wrap a handkerchief around the wound and fasten it with duct tape, as this can help dangerous bacteria grow over time.

K2 HOW TO CARVE—PART 1

Anyone who can handle the main piece of survival equipment —a knife—properly can make many more tools, weapons, shelter, etc., with it. This requires using the right cut and the right carving technique. If you have mastered this well the knife itself almost does not matter—it can also be a splinter of stone or a curved and sharpened tin can.

To practice cutting techniques, it is best to use a piece of sturdy hazel or dogwood as thick as your thumb; if you are very inexperienced linden is a suitable softwood.

BASIC CUT ▶

For all styles you use the knife in a similar manner: you cut or "saber" with it. The blade is not drawn across the wood like a plane, but is moved lengthwise. Otherwise the blade may get stuck fast and you will not get any farther.

◀ CUTTING WOOD

You can use a knife to cut down branches and small logs. You should not chop—a knife is not suitable for that—but cut through the wood after putting it under strain by bending it. At the sharpest point of the curve you push the blade into the fibers and they split as if by magic—the blade slips through as if through warm butter.

K2. HOW TO CARVE—PART 2

POWER CUT—FOR TRIMMING ▶

To make rough cuts with a lot of force, hold the blade so it points toward the base of your thumb and set the knife handle at a right angle to your breastbone **(A)**. Hold the wood to the blade from underneath. You can exert a lot of force by stretching your back muscles. You also have an exact overview of where you are carving. You can make precise cuts even in very hard wood.

A variation of trimming **(B)** is done by propping the knife on your knees by your shin and pulling the wood to be carved over the blade with your other hand. Again, you generate a lot of force, but the cut is not quite as precise.

You can learn how to carve a tent peg on page 63.

◀

▼ PRECISION CUT—FOR FINE CUTTING

If you take your knife in hand and place your thumb on the back of the blade, you can hold the wood underneath so there is also space for the thumb of your other hand on the blade.

This method lets you cut extremely fine slivers, down to about half a millimeter thick—which is important for making traps and producing tinder with a firesteel.

CROSS CUT—NOTCHES AND EDGES ▶

You especially have to cut across the grain when making traps or carving a barbed hook. You can do this by opening the blade and cutting through the wood using a light seesawing motion. Since this will not penetrate very deep you should combine this technique with precision cutting.

PUNCH CUT ▶

If you want to carve a hole or notch for mortising or joining, grip the knife right at the front of the blade. If the knife slips during carving any injury will be far less serious than if you hold the knife by the handle. Now you can stick the blade tip in the wood across the grain. Repeat this a centimeter away. You can now pull out the fibers in between.
OIf you want to make a hole in a piece of wood do the same on the other side until the two holes join in the middle.

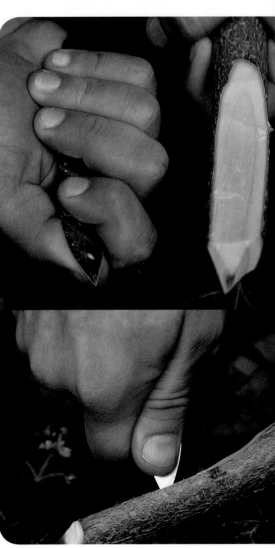

▼ CHOP CUT FOR A CLEAN FINISH

If one side of a branch should be cut cleanly, or you want to cut a slice from your salami, you can use a chop cut. Here you hold the knife quite far forward on the blade and use the thumb of the same hand to press the wood on to the blade. You have to make absolutely sure your thumb stays stretched and is far enough away from the cutting edge, otherwise you will cut yourself!

Carve your own eating utensils! Find out how on page 240.

▼

FIRE —
RESOURCE NO. 1

We assume that mankind has been using fire for at least 800,000 years. While the ancestors of modern humans still relied on lightning strikes and spontaneous fires, lighting a flame quickly became one of our most important survival skills.

By using marcasite and flint, by rubbing pieces of wood together, and later using matches and lighter, it was possible to light a fire fast to drive away wild animals, to illuminate caves, to warm themselves, or today, to prepare modern man's favorite dish: grilled meat.

Just to be able to stand around at a barbecue with your husband and not have to serve raw steaks, you should know and practice different methods for starting a fire.

F2. BLOWING ON A FIRE — GETTING FLAMES FROM EMBERS

Whether you drill, strike, or saw to make fire, the usual result is a small pile of glowing dust. To start a campfire, you must be able to turn this into flame. To do this, we use a fire nest of dry fibers.

To prepare the fire nest, you take some tinder the size of a hazel nut or walnut, such as cattail seeds or dandelion seeds, and squeeze them together a bit.

Put this small amount of tinder inside a slightly larger amount of very fine hay, bast fibers or something comparable, and press it all together.

Now look for the finest and driest grass you can find, braid it together, twist it a bit, and make a loop. Lay the tinder material you have already prepared in the resulting hollow. Now you can hold the braid like a torch.

When the fire nest is ready, put it aside and devote yourself to igniting the embers. When you have gotten this far, carefully place the embers you obtain in the center of the bundle. Before gathering up the fire nest, blow into the embers from above, to push them towards the tinder.

When the tinder in the fire nest has begun to glow, take it up, hold at an angle above your head, and blow as hard as you can and as directly on the embers as possible, until the fire nest, with a small burst, is aflame.

These tiny embers can turn into a great hot fire.

F3 FIRE HUT—IGNITE A FIRE SAFELY

Whether you are barbecuing in your garden, warming yourself in a cold forest, or starting a fire in the jungle, the start of a campfire is always the same: a small, basic fire. It is important to build a *small* fireplace, which makes it possible to first ignite fine material and bigger pieces always afterward. Especially in lousy weather, a small fire hut is an ideal way to safely start a campfire burning, even with just one match.

The purpose of the design is to create a chimney effect which lets existing flames spread rapidly to the rest of the fuel. You also have to protect your fuel—some of which must be carefully prepared—from the next downpour. To do this, recreate the basic construction of a → **debris hut** in miniature.

STEP 1 Fill the small frame—about twelve inches (thirty centimeters) in size—with some fine plant fibers, such as hay. These only need to flare up briefly to spread energy to the brushwood on top of them.

STEP 2 The brushwood layer should be about two to four inches (five to ten centimeters) thick. Put some pieces of wood no thicker than your thumb on top. It is best to break the sticks so they split open or fan out in a few places, increasing the surface area.

STEP 3 To protect the fire hut from rain you can cover it with bark or foliage. After the fire is ignited this cover will burn (even in the pouring rain).

If you don't have any fine plant fibers at hand, a tampon from one of your travel companions can be well-diverted for the purpose.

K3 THE ART OF ROPES— THE RIGHT BINDER

You will always need lines, cords, and ropes for survival. You can improvise some, but others you just have to take with you, since it is hard to find adequate replacements while traveling.

LINES AND ROPES

The general rule: There are **static lines** such as shoelaces, paracord **(A)**, cords **(B)**, belay rope or speleo rope **(C)**, and **dynamic ropes (D)** used in mountaineering. All have completely different purposes. Static ropes are used for → **rope bridges**, car towing, and for securing a load or lashing something down; mountaineering ropes are for belaying and rappelling.

If you use a static rope, or even a paracord, for mountaineering or rappelling, as opposed to a dynamic rope, it will brake you with a jolt. This results in an incredible impulse—sometimes a several-ton force—on the rope. This can break every bone in your body or break the rope.

If you go to the mountains or want to practice rappelling, you should definitely take a few yards of mountaineering rope.

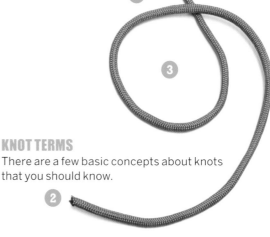

KNOT TERMS

There are a few basic concepts about knots that you should know.

LONG (1) AND SHORT (2) END Knots usually have a **long** and a **short end**. The long end is the side where the load is suspended, while the short is mostly used for knotting. This distinction is necessary because you can only put a load on some knots in one direction.

BIGHT (3) If you form a rope into a loop or a ring this makes a "bight." The simplest form of a bight is a curve or hairpin curve. To pull the rope "out of the bight" pull it from back to front through the loop.

HALF HITCH (4) For safety, always tie a knot leaving enough excess length behind the knot so that it does not come undone if a few inches should slip through the knot when it is pulled tight. Since the remaining end sometimes gets in the way or can get stuck somewhere, secure this short end usually with a half hitch, which is nothing more than knotting the rope to itself once.

▲
Example of a simple overhand knot: Tie the rope to a ring so that the short end (2) is above the long end (1). Then pull the short end from back to front through the bight (3). Secure the short end with a half hitch (4).

S1 CHOOSING YOUR CAMPSITE

Since living in a makeshift shelter requires large amounts of natural resources and you will be exposed to the weather anyway, in principle, wooded or overgrown areas are especially suitable sites. But remember, in an emergency, it will be hard for search teams to find you in the forest from an airplane, so you should set up your forest camp at the edge of a clearing so you can quickly reach an open area.

You can find large amounts of firewood, food, water, and protection from wind in the forest, but trees also represent a potential hazard. During thunderstorms you are safe in the woods from the driving rain, but at risk from falling trees, breaking branches, or a lightning strike. You may be able to find a natural wind barrier, such as the roots of a fallen tree trunk or a thicket of young trees.

Exposed hilltops near particularly tall or decayed trees and depressions are unsuitable places. The latter can fill up with water when it rains, valleys can be flooded, and rivers overflow their banks. In the immediate vicinity of a body of water, mornings can also be made uncomfortably clammy by fog. So you should keep some distance from water, but on the other hand not be so far away that it takes hours to get drinking water. Your ideal surface should be flat and dry.

There is no "perfect" campsite. It is worthwhile to weigh the various arguments for and against a particular place because you might be spending some time there.

M2 TRANSPORTING AN INJURED PERSON

If you have to transport a travel partner for a long distance over difficult terrain it is best to use the "fireman's carry." First lay the patient down, positioned as well as possible, then load them over your shoulders and drape them around your neck like a fox fur.

If the position is properly balanced you can carry them down steep slopes or through rivers without having to hold the transported person too tightly. If your travel partner is still conscious they can hold on at the knees.

By using the fireman's carry, in an emergency you can even carry someone with a broken foot or the like for long distances. **When lifting, it is important to keep your back straight to prevent injuring yourself.**

Boreal forests and your native forest are great for survival training. Here you find an extreme diversity of potential materials, edible plants and animals, and the opportunity to pursue your hobby out of sight (and in peace). As familiar as this environment seems to you, there are still some dangers and special features for which you should prepare yourself.

SURVIVAL IN THE FOREST

The Undergrowth

A few feet away from the nearest trail, separated by an impenetrable blackberry thicket, the forest opens up. There are still dense green islands, even in the immediate vicinity of many cities, that let us forget the stress of everyday life for a short time.

It is a gateway to a strange world, where the sultry heat gives way to the damp shade of dense treetops.

In Europe and North America everyone is entitled to go into the forest for recreation and sports. It is a matter of honor for a forest hiker that they do not leave any trace of their presence behind in the woods after survival training.

E11 FOREST HIKER EQUIPMENT

You can find everything you need to survive in forests. Your equipment for this region should be light and sturdy enough that you can carry it in a backpack that will not get torn by brambles. This is the place for cotton camouflage pants, wrought iron hatchets, and waxed raincoats.

For living and survival in the forest, a lot revolves around using natural materials and splitting wood. The combination of a lightweight knife with a small ax is actually easier to use than a large knife; in addition, it is often lighter.

Muted colored clothing not only makes it possible to train undisturbed, but is also key for watching wildlife.

Canteen: For carrying drinking water and preparing food, a sturdy canteen/ cookware combo is the right choice. ▶

Camouflage pants: Heavy cotton fabric not only protects you from thorns, but also provides some protection against cuts. ◀

Folding saw: If you have to split wood into usable pieces a knife will not go very far, but a folding pruning saw does. ◀

Hatchet: The hatchet is the ax's little sister. Use it to split kindling and clear annoying undergrowth. ▶

R5 STINGING NETTLES: OIL RICH NUTS

The stinging nettle is a plant between twenty-seven to fifty-nine inches (seventy and 150 centimeters) tall with decussate, saw-edged leaves. The blossoms spring out between leaf and stem. Nettles are easy to recognize by their unpleasant stinging hairs.

If you bend a nettle over, the woody inner part remains hanging on a tough, often reddish bast which can be used for making → **cords**.

Nettles are often found in large fields. The plant is dioecious—that is, that there are female and male plants. **While the female blossoms contain oil-rich nutlets starting in early summer, the male flowers provide little energy.**

The leaves can be prepared by simply stripping off the stinging hairs "along the line of growth" to be eaten raw. The poison-loaded hollow stinging tubes break off during this process. Some plants from the stinging nettle family that grow in tropical regions have a very strong irritant effect.

0.4 in.
(1 cm.)

S2 MAKING A SIMPLE FIELD MATTRESS

Because creepy crawlies come to visit you in the dark, making a simple camping mat of wood and scrub makes sense. This lets you lie down raised a little above the floor.

To construct it, lay three logs down crosswise at a distance depending on your body length. Fill the resulting spaces with foliage, brush, and grass. Now you can lay long poles lengthwise to the first ones on the frame. Then comes cushioning material.

Such a bed can be a comfortable place to sleep, even at very low temperatures.

K4 HOW TO MAKE CORDS

For making a trap, if your laces are torn, for making a fire drill, or for repairing equipment, improvised cords can be very helpful.

First, look for suitable fibers. You can get bast from lindens, black locust, willow, and many other trees, or from the fibrous layer of plants like nettles or burdock. The fibers should be strips as long as possible and between $^3/_{64}$ and $^{13}/_{64}$ in. (one and five millimeters) wide.

To make a long cord that is consistently strong bend back the first piece of fiber off the middle and hold it like a hairpin. Now turn the two juxtaposed partial strands in the same direction without laying them atop **(1)** each other. This produces a twist in the fibers which turns them into a cord. When you get to the end of a fiber, add the next fiber and twist it into the cord **(2)**. Secure the end with a simple knot.

1 ◀ When making cords both fibers must be turned in the same direction.

2 ◀ Extend the end of the fiber by twisting in a new piece with some overlap.

48

F4 DRILLING A FIRE LIKE A PRO

FIRE DRILL KIT To drill a fire you need a strong cord, a bow, a spindle made of hardwood (hazel), a plank of soft wood (spruce, poplar, or linden), and a fireboard of stone or hard wood.

Bow: The simplest form for the beginner is a forked branch. ▼

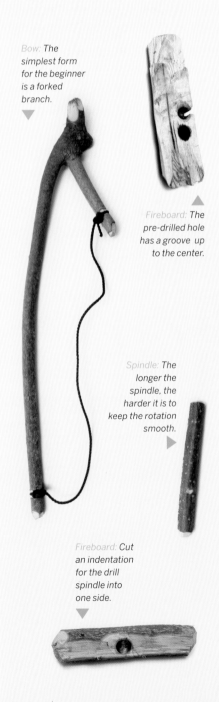

▲ *Fireboard: The pre-drilled hole has a groove up to the center.*

Spindle: The longer the spindle, the harder it is to keep the rotation smooth. ▶

Fireboard: Cut an indentation for the drill spindle into one side. ▼

ASSEMBLING A FIRE DRILL
Knot the cord loosely into the bow. Twist the cord around the spindle. "Smear" the fireboard with some grass and set the spindle on it. If you move the spindle by the cord it rotates by itself.

GENERATING EMBERS
When drilling a fire the result is always carbon dust which begins to glow. If you see on television flames arising from the drilling you know this is cheating. How to do it correctly:

When drilling, the softwood board must be absolutely stable, then black wood powder accumulates in a heap in the groove.

▼

STEP 1 Cut an indentation into the board.

STEP 2 Use the fire drill to bore this indentation into a small hole that forms a groove. The hot wood powder "flows" through this.

STEP 3 Put some dry plant fibers or cotton beneath the groove. The hot wood dust collects there.

STEP 4 Now keep boring with great force at high speed as long as needed until you get a black heap of dust the size of a hazelnut.

STEP 5 Bring the dust heap to a glow by fanning or blowing on it and place it in a tinder nest. More at → **blowing on a fire**.

2 + 3

4

5

49

R6 RECOGNIZE EDIBLE TREES

If you are able to recognize and
distinguish the main edible trees
you can always find something to
eat in temperate zone forests all
over the world.

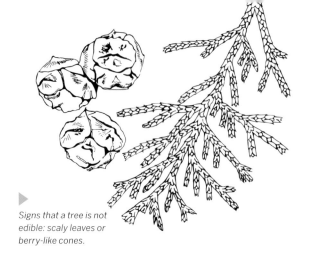

▶ Signs that a tree is not
edible: scaly leaves or
berry-like cones.

CONIFERS

There are three large groups of
conifers: **pines**, the **yew type**, and
the **cypress type**. While pine type
trees, such as cedar, spruce, and
pine, are edible, you can poison
yourself by eating deadly yew and
cypress type conifers.

To distinguish among these three
groups you should pay attention to
the needles and cones. If the tree has
needles *and* cones like a typical fir
tree, it is almost certainly one of the

*In a typical coniferous
forest ❶ you almost
always find something
to eat. Even juicy yew
"berries" ❷ are
edible; the seeds,
however, are highly
toxic. With a pine
cone ❸ it is hard
to go wrong.*
▼

pines. You can eat the seeds from the
cones roasted or raw. If the tree has
normal cones *but* scale-like leaves
(thuja, cypress), or real needles
but berry-like cones or fruits
(juniper, yew), for safety you
should not use them. **If you are sure
you recognize the yew, the red,
juicy flesh can be eaten, but the
seeds are still highly toxic.**

Before cooking, give chestnuts a light crosswise cut with a knife. They can be fried in oil or roasted directly in the embers. If you eat large amounts raw they can cause vomiting.

BROAD-LEAFED TREES

If you have found a deciduous tree that has undivided, "simple" leaves (not shaped like a hand) and dark brown round or three-sided fruits with a prickly shell you can assume it is an oak, beech, or edible chestnut type.

In the temperate and cold regions there are many different types of these edible plants all over the world. To avoid confusion, you should note that horse chestnuts, which have a similar fruit, but hand-shaped leaves, do not belong to this group.

If you want to consume large quantities of these oil-rich acorns, beechnuts, and chestnuts they should be roasted.

If they are still bitter, chop them up and immerse them in a net in water for a while. This leaches out the bitter substances.

Edible chestnuts never have hand-shaped foliage. The shell is uncomfortably prickly.

▼

Edible until early summer: Beechnuts (left) and acorns (right) from the past autumn.

▼

W3 FINDING WATER IN THE FOREST

If you are in search of drinking water in the woods you should look for ferns, mosses, and horsetails. These plants usually only grow in wet locations.

Rushes often indicate a waterlogged place in the woods. If the ground is only damp, if need be, you can press water out through a cloth.

Other ways to find water include → **distilling earth** and consuming soil that is clean.

The water is extracted in the intestine and the loam is excreted. You should not do this for any length of time because the loam can limit absorption of certain nutrients.

In the spring, you can cut off the bark of edible broad-leaf trees. The sugary sap, which never contains dangerous bacteria, flows out.

GET ORIENTED AND SET YOUR MARCHING DIRECTION

Topographical maps are often used for navigation by compass. Since you do not need any batteries for this way of getting oriented and setting your marching direction, in many places it is preferable to a GPS and should be taken along as a backup.

Since maps only represent a two-dimensional approximation of your surroundings, be particularly sure you use precise maps and exercise great care when navigating.

GET ORIENTED While the grid lines on a map lead to the geographic North Pole, the tip of the compass needle points to magnetic north. As a result, depending on where you are traveling, a more or less strong declination can arise. You must take this into consideration when orienting the map. This is either recorded on the map by a combination arrow (True North/Map North) or as a declination in degrees. To do this, turn the case or indicator so the North imprint is at the top. Lay the compass on the grid line and turn everything around until the compass needle indicates the declination value, or with a negative declination, the value 360 minus the western declination. Now the map depicts your surroundings.

SET YOUR MARCHING DIRECTION To get your bearings from a known standpoint to a goal, put the compass on the oriented map on a connecting line between the standpoint **(A)** and destination point **(B)**. Spin the indicator so the North imprint **(C)** matches the compass needle. Take the direction the compass shows when the compass needle covers the indicator arrow.

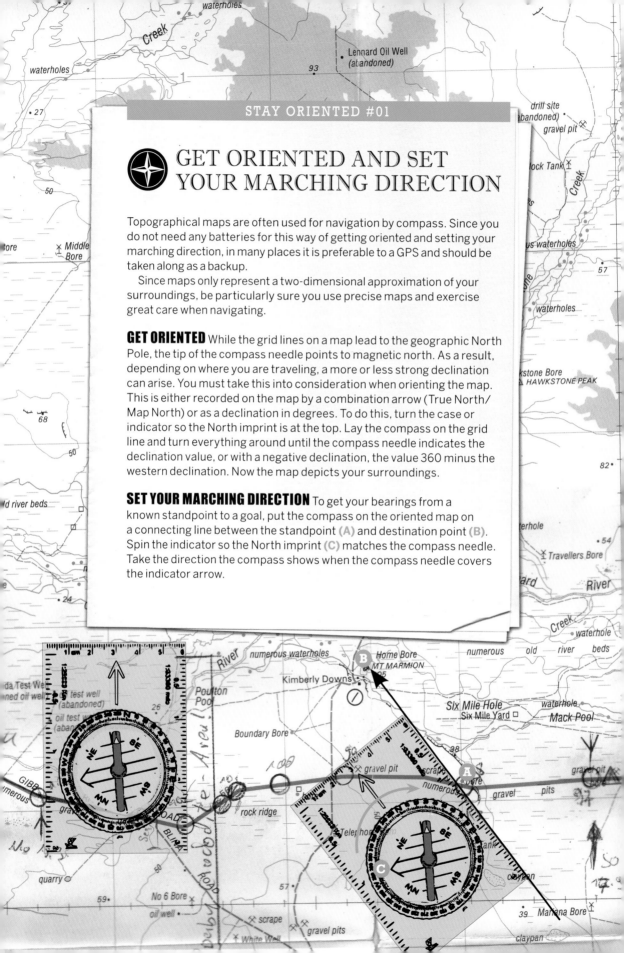

K·5 SIGNAL FIRE

While in the mountains, ground-to-air signals—and in the desert or on water, light reflections—are often sufficient to make yourself seen, but all the structures in a forest can prevent vehicles, let alone individuals, from being seen. If possible, **you should look for a clearing or a lake shore to build a signal pyramid.**

Since leaves and needles are rather dark, it is advisable to use smoke fumes to draw attention. Until you have finished your signal pyramid you can stack straw or moss by the fire so you can throw it on immediately if a vehicle comes into view.

STEP 1 Construct a frame from wood like an equilateral pyramid. Halfway up make a platform to put smoke-making material.

STEP 2 Loosely stack very dry fuel under the platform. It must be done so that it burns very quickly.

STEP 3 Place green, damp plant materials loosely on top. Cover everything with a rain-resistant layer of leaves or foil.

STEP 4 If you now touch a flame to the signal pyramid and enlarge it by blowing air on it, the fire material works as a propellant and flares up in a few seconds, pushing moisture and soot toward the layer of plant material above. In a few moments a dense, white column of smoke develops which is visible for miles.

A small fire pyramid can be built quickly and can produce a dense, white plume of smoke very efficiently and in a short time.

K6 MAKE A SLINGSHOT

The slingshot is one of the most effective hunting weapons for short distances. A slingshot makes it possible to throw stones at a high speed, so that in an emergency you can exactly strike and kill small animals like birds or squirrels. Often the animals are knocked unconscious or cannot fly for a short time, which is why you should take a long stick as a club along when hunting with a slingshot. As materials, you need something elastic, such as some condoms or a waistband, a forked branch, and some leather or bark for the pocket.

Fasten the elastic on with line wound around the stick (using for example → **fishing knots**), or attach

You can make a slingshot with a forked branch, some bark, and an elastic band. ▼

it with a noose. Make holes in the leather through which the elastic band is threaded and attached. **To hit your target with the slingshot you have to practice.** There is no sure way to aim here as there is with a gun. When hunting, aim based on practice through pure guesswork.

F5 FEATHER STICKS— THE FIRE STARTER

In the forest it can be difficult to find dry wood to light after several days of rain. It is especially hard to burn brushwood which has lain on the ground or in the water for several weeks. In this case you can make so-called feather sticks. To do this, look for wood that is not decayed yet and cut it around with a → **precision cut** so that you get several hundred fine curls. When you have made about ten of these feather sticks place them in the → **fire hut.** If the curls are fine enough you can even get green wood to burn. This technique is also ideal in the rainforest.

R7 EATING ROSES

Roses grow in hedges or as creepers which spread at the edge of woods with extraordinary speed. The bloom usually shows radial symmetry, has five or ten petals, and an enlarged green calyx. All woody parts of these plants are covered with what can be aggressive thorns. The leaves are pinnate and have a serrated edge. The fruit is the rose hip, which look like small apples. The color of the fruit—filled with many seeds—ranges from red-orange to pink.

If you want to eat larger amounts of the seeds you should roast them, because they contain **heat-sensitive cyanide compounds.** You can singe the hairs on the seeds—known as "itching powder"—during the roasting process by rolling a big ember over the seeds.

Rose hip tea can help relieve colds. A brew from the leaves is used for throat infections.

◀

All parts of roses are edible. The safest way for you to recognize the rose is by the rose hips and thorns. When you roast rose hips the poisonous cyanide compounds are destroyed.

W4 DRINKING WATER FROM PLANTS AND STUMPS

You can often get water from plants with broad foliage even days after the last rain. Water can also be found in stumps and knot holes some days after the last rain. Note that such water can be contaminated with bird droppings or insects which have fallen in, so boil the water if possible.

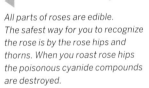

Open water holes are often used by animals as drinking troughs.

▼

R8 A WELL-SPREAD TABLE— DEADWOOD AS A FOOD SOURCE

Whatever may be often claimed, you can't get any energy from wood—except sometimes from plant sap. Even the cambium (a soft layer of cells in the cortex) has practically no energy. Humans and most animals are unable to digest cellulose.

Insects, however, are adapted to burrow tunnels through wood and to break down shredded wood pulp using bacteria.

If you are looking for food in the forest, you will almost always be able to find a meal in or under deadwood. To do this you first peel the bark from the trunk, and underneath you often find something delicious, like wood lice and the fat white larvae of wood beetles. If there is nothing there use a piece of wood to scrape out a layer from decaying, not-too-wet wood from the core. Use a pointed object such as a thorn to extract woodworms from their burrows.

When you have "harvested" the trunk and moved it from its place you will immediately find food, including larvae, which live on fungi under the roots; and complete ant and mice nests that use the heavy cover as a shelter.

Where there is deadwood there is also something to eat.

W5 DISTILLING EARTH

To get water from damp mud and to make urine, salt water, or dirty water definitely drinkable you can distill the liquid. The water turns to steam on one side of the distillation unit and is condensed back on the other side as clean and clear water. You can improvise a distillation unit by connecting a bottle with a heat-resistant hose to water and heating it. It is important when using a long bottle to add a little sand or a few stones. Overloading can lead to "delayed boiling" and that can cause → **combustion**. You can also improvise a distillation unit with a pot and cover by setting the cover slightly askew, but

If you set the pot lid askew during cooking you can catch distilled water.

a lot of steam will be lost. For best results use a tube which is passed through cold water. But you should not distill anything alcoholic with such a distillation unit—the heat

cannot be adjusted cleanly without a thermometer, and therefore the distillate captured as foreshot and feint will have headache potential.

K7 COOKING WITHOUT POTS

If you are outdoors without a pot or pan and have to boil water, or if you want to prepare some greens, you can do so using inverse cooking. Dig yourself a little pit in the ground and cover the sides with some waterproof foil or large leaves. Alternatively, you can also cook in a bowl. Pour the soup or water into it. Heat some stones in a fire. Now roll them or put them into the water, one after another, using → **barbeque tongs**. At first the stones are quenched with a hiss, but after a short time the water begins to boil actively. If food is to be cooked longer, cover the pit after it has begun to boil and let each stone remain in the water at least five minutes.

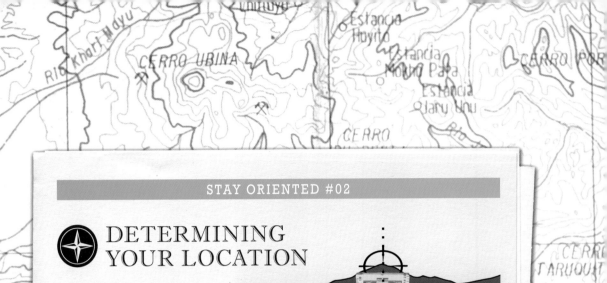

DETERMINING YOUR LOCATION

If you have a map and compass but are not sure where you are, you can quite easily determine your location by getting your bearings.

STEP 1 To do this, lay the map on the ground and →**orient it**. Now look for a distinctive mountain, tower, or hill and get the bearing with the compass. Read the number of degrees or mark the direction North by turning the case and lay the compass on the map.

STEP 2 Now lay it with an edge on the target for your bearing and turn it so that it again stands exactly where it was when just getting the bearing. Draw a line.

STEP 3 Repeat the process with a second distinctive point—ideally standing at a right angle to the first target point. The point of intersection of these two lines is your current location. If you want to make sure, you can check this with a third bearing.

You can use a normal map compass to get a bearing. You need to plot at least two bearings to determine your own standpoint (red dot) on the map.

R9 FUNGI AS EMERGENCY RATIONS?

Even if you like to collect mushrooms in your local woods, in unknown regions they are not a suitable emergency food. Even if you think you can correctly identify or recognize a mushroom, this does not mean it is fit for human consumption in the place where you happen to be. Local varieties of individual types make it almost impossible to identify mushrooms safely everywhere, especially since they often have poisonous "doppelgangers." The scientific community is still not unanimous on whether many fungi are edible or not.

Therefore, you should not rely on fungi as an emergency food. This is no great loss, except for the taste. Mushrooms have virtually no nutritional value; they mainly consist of indigestible chitin and water. Mushrooms have thus even significantly less nutritional value than the leaves of green plants.

K8 SHARPENING KNIVES AND HATCHETS

If you frequently use your knife or hatchet outdoors over a longer period you should sharpen it regularly. Look for the flattest and smoothest stone you can find, then wet it with saliva, and rub it smooth with a second stone until the entire working surface is covered with a tough, gray, metallic-smelling mass.

Do the **first polish (1)** with this stone by drawing the blade over it, with the edge held flat, changing sides thirty to forty times using light pressure in the direction of the edge. Then spread some of the paste on a flat piece of wood and draw the blade over this another thirty times.

For a **fine polish (2)**, look for a horsetail, divide it into sections as long as possible, and arrange them parallel to each other. Flatten the top surface slightly and use as described above for polishing.

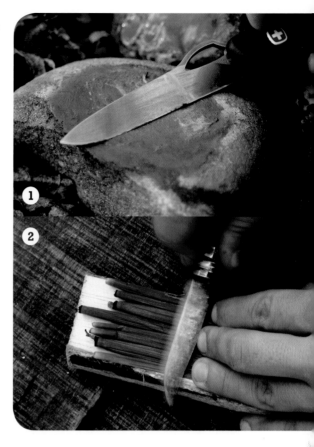

S3 HOW TO CARVE A TENT PEG

Tent spikes and pegs are items you are likely to lose on the forest floor or forget at home. You can carve a complete tent peg in less than a minute from a piece of branch.

Use the → **power cut** to carve along the length of the wood and to carve a four-sided pointed tip on one side (1). Carve the edges by twisting the peg 90°. On the other side, use the → **chop cut** (2) to carve a smooth surface to drive into the ground. Now comes the hook: Carve the blunt side of the branch in a cross shape using the → **cross cut** (3), then carve away three of the four resulting surfaces using the → **precision cut** (4). The tent peg is done.

▲
A carved wooden tent peg is at least as good as any you can buy in terms of stability and resilience.

▲
You will find these carving techniques in Survival Basics starting on page 33.

S4 A MAKESHIFT SHELTER OF BRANCHES AND LEAVES

A debris hut is the classic woodland hiker's hut. To build one you need a lot of dry leaves, lumber, and quite a bit of time.

Think of a debris hut as a small ridge tent which extends into the ground at the foot side. Since it is an enclosed construction, the interior must be just big enough to give you enough space.

A debris hut is made from a base frame covered and insulated with twigs, leaves, and moss.

The bigger the hut the colder it will be inside during the night.

BUILDING MATERIALS Forked branches for a roof ridge slightly taller than your height, a lot of branches, and covering material such as leaves, twigs, moss, etc.

STEP 1 First use the forked branches and long beams to build the basic structure: Stick the forked branch into the ground and set the long beams at an angle into it, so that you can lie underneath without bumping into it with your feet or head.

STEP 2 Now lay a lot of sticks and twigs on top on both sides, close together and parallel to the ridge. This will build up both roof surfaces at the same time. The steeper it all is the better water will flow off. If the roof slope is too steep the roofing material could slide off.

STEP 3 To finish it off, spread masses of dry leaves—in an emergency even wet leaves mixed with stalks, twigs, and moss—over the floor surface. The more the better. A thick layer also keeps you warmer. The best is to first cover the back area, then work toward the front.

After finishing the debris hut crawl in feet first and close the door with rescue foil or brushwood.

IMPORTANT: Never start a fire in a debris hut, including with charcoal—there is a risk of suffocation!

M3 WHO'S AFRAID OF THE FOX TAPEWORM?

When collecting edible wild plants in the forest there is a risk you can be infected with parasite eggs. For example, if a dog has lifted his leg in a nettle field just before you harvest your greens there.

When estimating the risk, do not forget that even store-bought vegetables come from fields that are not fenced in. Theoretically, any plant from the vegetable stand can be infected with a parasite—but this happens only rarely.

In contrast, the fox tapeworm is a concern for wild plant collectors in temperate forests (North America and central Europe). We know, according to current information, that people infected with the fox tapeworm do not get it by consuming contaminated berries or herbs, but from eggs which have been dispersed and inhaled—for example, when skinning a fox.

The likelihood that just a few hours before you arrive a fox or other infected animal has answered the call of nature exactly on the wild plants you want to pick is also very low. Personally, I would nevertheless not pick my "wild lettuce" in any park which is particularly popular as a dog exercise area.
Basically: All plant foods can be safely consumed once they have been scalded.

▲
You can get tapeworms like these shown here by eating wild herbs, but not the fox tapeworm.

M4 REMOVE TICKS SAFELY

Ticks are common parasites of humans. If you go walking in the woods you will almost always find a few on your body.

Ticks transmit many different diseases worldwide. Most pathogens are transmitted only after the tick has been sucking on the host for a few hours. It is therefore important they be found quickly and removed. You should not manipulate around the insect using any homemade "wooden tweezers." This only increases the risk that the tick will leave its infectious gut contents in the wound. The same goes for resin, which is often applied to the tick to smother it.

Ticks can easily be removed with a knife. To do this, slip the knife from behind under the tick, as if you wanted to shave it away. Then hold the rear part of the tick carefully with your thumb and pull the tick, with a twisting motion, out of your body over the back of the knife.

Even if a piece of the proboscis remains stuck it will be ejected from the top layer of skin in a few days.

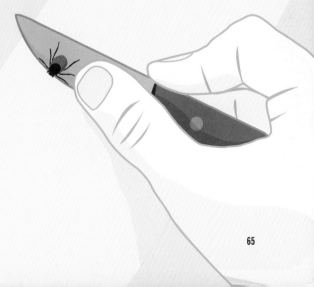

CLOVE HITCH

If you have to fasten a rope around a pole or mast, the clove hitch is the right choice. With this knot you can drag wood through the forest and secure logs when constructing a temporary shelter.

STEP 1 Put the rope around the pole, leaving an excess length. The long end should be held at an angle.

STEP 2 Pull the short end up so that it crosses the long end. Wrap the short end once more around the attachment point.

STEP 3 A small opening is formed at the crossover point of the rope. Thread the rope through this. Tighten the knot.

STEP 4 If the knot should be tighter you can repeat steps two and three as often as you want.

IMPORTANT: If the fixing point, such as a mast, can turn, the knot can unwind and untie the securing point. This knot is not suited for securing a person!

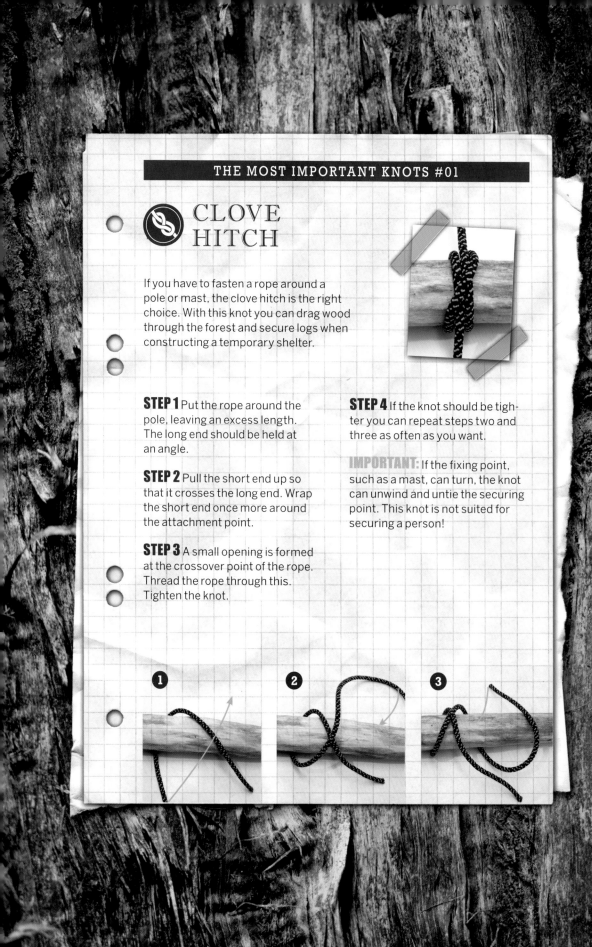

R10 PAJUTE DEATH TRAP

The Pajute death trap is ideal to catch small animals such as rats and squirrels. With a little practice you can build one in a few minutes. Cut two sticks about twelve inches (30 centimeters) long. Give one of them a flat tip using the precision cut **(A)**; make a notch in the top quarter of the other **(B)** by alternating the precision and cross cut.

Bind a piece of paracord or → **improvised cord (C)** to its end. At the height of the notch knot a small piece of wood **(D)** into the cord.

Drive the piece with the flat tip into the ground, then set the wood with the notch on top. Load the impact weight (at least four times the animal's body weight, preferably more) on the tip **(E)**. Wind around the sticks once again to the upright stick with the cord and fasten

it with a thin wooden trigger **(F)**, on which you put the bait. The lightest touch will trigger the trap and the weight whizzes down and kills the animal.

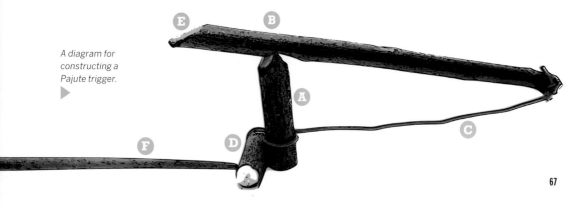

A diagram for constructing a Pajute trigger.
▶

Many people seek relaxation by hiking and alpine rock climbing in the mountains. The barren environment above the tree line not only offers a change from the densely populated city, but is also particularly dangerous due to high altitude, solar radiation, and exposure to the elements. Rockfalls, avalanches, and storms are just a few examples of the problems for which you should prepare yourself.

SURVIVAL IN THE
MOUNTAINS

Freedom

With every meter I climb higher, the air is clearer. The haze of the valley already lies far below me. The summit still appears to be unreachably far away. Breathing is increasingly difficult. The glaring sun is reflected from millions of tiny snow mirrors and stings my eyes. My feet hurt, and every step is a struggle.

And yet the summit develops a power of attraction that I can barely resist.

E12 MOUNTAIN EQUIPMENT

In a survival situation, it is important to descend from high altitudes as soon as possible, to at least below the tree line. Thin air and rapidly changing weather conditions, coupled with deep precipices, glaring light →**alpine sun**, and insurmountable steep surfaces make the mountains a dangerous region. To be able to get out of the danger zone quickly, and in an emergency spend the night in the mountains, it is especially important to carry safety equipment and a very lightweight pack.

Mountaineers often take too little equipment along when "storming the summit," and this can lead to life-threatening situations.

The most important pieces of equipment you need to rescue yourself in high altitudes will fit in a small day backpack, including, **besides suitable clothing and sunscreen**, the following equipment:

▶ *Bivy sack: If the weather suddenly gets so bad you cannot continue forward a bivy sack can save your life.*

▲
Climbing rope:
*A →**dynamic rope** with a sturdy and abrasion resistant coating helps when you are surmounting a deep abyss.*

Express slings: Two carabiners, connected to a belt loop, help you secure yourself when climbing and as a fixed point for rappelling.
◀

Lap belt: A light lap belt is the ideal solution for fastening on the rope to secure it when traversing or descending.
▼

HMS carabiner: When rappelling down cliffs you need a hook you can close.
◀

72

K9 SHIFTING WEATHER IN THE MOUNTAINS

If you are hiking in the mountains, you have to be constantly on the lookout for the weather. Sunshine can turn into a storm within the briefest time. If you are already hanging on a wall when this happens it can be very unpleasant. Basically, there are three important cloud formations for making an assessment:

CIRRUS — FEATHERY CLOUDS [1] These consist of very fine ice particles in high-altitude air layers. If they are the only clouds in the sky, this indicates that the weather is fairly stable.

CUMULUS HUMILIS — FAIR-WEATHER CLOUDS [2]
At peaks the wind is drawn upward. This makes light, damp air rise, which then condenses in the cold layers. Therefore, fair-weather clouds often gather directly above a summit. It is important that they are sharply defined above and below.

CUMULONIMBUS — THUNDERHEADS [3] When thunderheads appear, which can also quickly develop from disintegrating fair-weather clouds, the humid air is piling up at high altitudes. Therefore, the clouds usually appear very dark underneath. This means highest level alert: Things are going to break loose soon.

K10 THE BIGGEST MISTAKES IN MOUNTAIN HIKING

A common saying is, "Mountains don't forgive any mistakes." But if the mountains were actually so grim many more hikers would find their graves on an airy height. Nevertheless, climbing a mountain, whether 1,640 or 16,400 ft. (500 or 5,000 m.) above sea level, is always dangerous. Here it is not falling rocks and high-altitude air which pose the greatest risk, but **overconfidence and lack of experience**.

Any mountain newbie with no snow or alpine experience, with an inadequate or too-heavy pack, who plans to cross mountains in winter is as doomed to fail as the vacationer who wants to climb a mountain in sandals with a walking stick but no safety equipment. Anyone who cannot assess their own condition, who misjudges their own capabilities and knowledge, is in danger in any mountain situation.

If you are drawn to the mountains, you should start in the hills outside your front door. The techniques you need in the mountains are the same that you can practice on a slight incline. You can also learn how to secure yourself and rappelling and rescue from heights from a mountaineering club, or from equipment manufacturers.

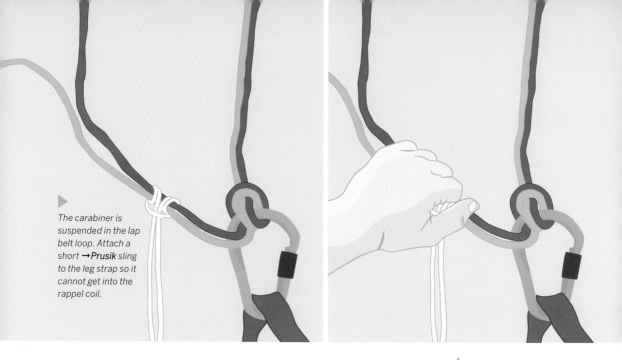

▶ The carabiner is suspended in the lap belt loop. Attach a short → *Prusik* sling to the leg strap so it cannot get into the rappel coil.

K11 RAPPELING METHODS AND WHAT TO WATCH FOR

▲ Carry the Prusik knot along in your braking hand when rappelling. If you accidentally let go of the rope, the knot locks it and prevents a fall.

When you stand, with all your equipment, on an abyss blocking your descent, you still have to get down any way you can.

The technique you need here is rappelling. Take note that you should **never** do this using a static—that is, inelastic—paracord. While this will hold your body weight without a problem, one small jerk due to a slip could be enough to tear the cord, because the impulse can generate several hundred pounds of strain. It is safest to rappel with a dynamic (elastic) → **mountain rope**. Generally, the rope is wrapped around a tree trunk or anchored firmly on rocks (for example, use a hook or a → **monkey's fist knot**) and then extended downward doubled. The rope must never be pulled through a sharp-edged opening or a rope loop when carrying a load. You rappel on both lines—when you are down, you can pull the rope down and pack it up again.

RAPPELLING OVER AN EDGE ▶

For rappelling, make the rope taut and bend your knees a bit. Standing backward to the edge, you let yourself down slowly over the edge and let out the rope very slowly. Even before you are at a right angle make a step back and you are now on the wall. Now it is best to rappel in small steps. Although jumping while releasing at the same time does look better, there is always the associated risk that you will twist and hit your head against the wall.

There are two methods for rappelling: the *safe* and the *improvised unsafe* method.

SAFE: RAPPELLING WITH CARIBINER AND HARNESS ▷

Fasten a fixable carabiner on your harness. Using a doubled rope, tie a munter hitch (crossing hitch). Take care here that the "securing side" of the carabiner opening is averted or the screw connection may otherwise be loosened.

Now tie a piece of paracord to the → **prusik**, pull it over both ropes, and fasten it to the carabiner. When rappelling, the "securing side" of the rope is held under tension and slows down your sliding. Simultaneously pull along the prusik knot. When slipping, if you let completely loose of the "securing side" the prusik brakes you and prevents a fall.

UNSAFE: THE DÜLFER SEAT ▷

Rappelling with the Dülfer seat is generally done on a slope, but not on a steep wall. Here, the doubled rope is first fastened from the front between the legs under one thigh. Now cross rope once over your chest, and pass again back over your shoulder to your side, and secure it there with your hand. Slowly let the rope slip through your hand —it brakes you by being wound around your body. Incidentally, this is just as painful as it sounds. When using the Dülfer seat, you must never slide from the rock with your feet, because the rope might unwind and let you fall.

When rappelling over the edge you should avoid making big jumps as much as possible.

INTERPRETING CONTOUR LINES

If you are looking for a safe way through the mountains, it is important to be able to interpret contour lines correctly.

On maps, the landscape is displayed in two dimensions. Altitudes cannot be shown in relief, but so-called contour lines indicate how steep the slope is and how high a mountain is. There are typical contour lines that you should recognize.

Any one contour line on a map always indicates the same altitude. If you are following a line, you are moving along one level.

LINE THICKNESS You find contour lines on a map in two line widths. The thicker lines (A) show mostly to a round value, such as 3,000, 3,500, and 4,000 meters altitude. In between are uniformly distributed thinner lines (B), which indicate the slope in, for example, 100th or 200th increments.

VERY CLOSE LINES indicate a very steep slope (C). Avoid it if possible.

WIDESPREAD LINES If the slope is very slight (D), the farther the lines are apart, the less slope to the terrain.

FOLDED BACK HAIRPIN CURVES indicate a gorge (E), where the inner contour lines are lower down. If the inner contours are higher up, in contrast, this indicates the structure of a steep ridge (F).

LINES THAT WIND OVER SEVERAL SUMMITS This indicates a high plateau with peaks or valleys lying on it (G). It is possible to find a way through such terrain without having to ascend or descend (traversing).

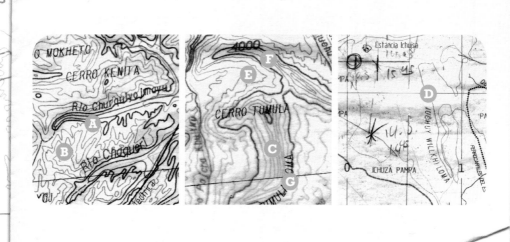

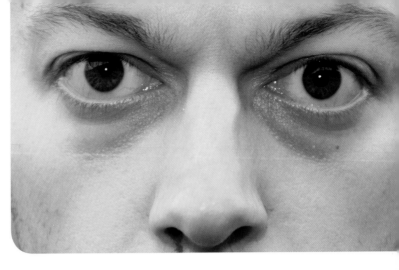

If the pupils are different sizes it is an important sign of a hemorrhage or accumulation of water in the skull. A skull fracture can be accompanied by bleeding from the nose, mouth, and ears.

M5 BRAIN CONCUSSION

If you fall when rope climbing you may hit your head against the wall. This can happen even if you wear a helmet. The result is a head injury—a concussion.

A serious head injury can cause hemorrhaging in the skull. This creates pressure on nerve tissue. As a result, respiration and blood pressure can become unbalanced—**in severe cases leading to respiratory arrest or death from a circulatory collapse**.

But it can also happen that—as when a knocked-out boxer recovers—these vital functions are restored in a few minutes. However, bleeding can also increase pressure in the skull slowly, leading to a delayed blackout.

A patient with traumatic brain injury must be constantly monitored. If they are conscious they should keep their eyes open. This way, if the pupils show a different diameter, you can quickly see that pressure is building up in the head. Other signals include nausea, vomiting, limited consciousness to unconsciousness, and circulatory changes. Quite certain indications are different light reactions in the pupils and irregular breathing.

The injured person should be positioned with the head elevated to reduce blood pressure in the skull. If breathing or heartbeat collapse start cardiopulmonary resuscitation immediately.

ATTENTION: In case of headache, under no circumstances give aspirin or other blood-thinning agents!

K12 HIGH-ALTITUDE COOKING

If you are hiking above the tree line, you usually will not find enough fuel to make a fire. Sometimes you find lichens and moss, but rarely enough to cook efficiently in a hobo oven.

If you know before starting out that you will be going through areas that have little woodland, you should either take enough fuel along the way or carry along a light gas stove, which can be used to melt snow and prepare food.

R11 FOXTAILS

The amaranth, or "foxtail," is among the most robust "weeds." Most herbaceous plants have alternating or opposite leaves. The leaves are usually exstipulate, and most are oval-shaped, sometimes a pointed oval. The often green, sometimes purple flowers stand up like flaky and dense "foxtails" in the upper leaf axils. The lower stem portion is often reddish and broadens out like a turnip. The green leafy parts of amaranth smell a bit like spinach; the lower part smells like sugar beet. Some foxtail species were the staple food of entire civilizations in South America—today the seeds have found their way into our food stores as "kiwicha." They can be found literally anywhere, even above the tree line. Their main distribution area is the tropics, but you can also find many plants of this genus right on your doorstep.

The leaves of foxtails are similar to spinach; they are very closely related.
▶

K13 CLIMBING BACK UP

If you have fallen into a crevasse or want to get back up after → **rappelling**, you have to climb up the free-hanging rope. This is not so easy on a steep wall, especially with a heavy backpack hanging on your back. In this situation the prusik technique is used. To do this, you knot two loops for your feet into two pieces of paracord or laces about three feet (one meter) long (→ **bowline** or → **figure eight knots**), as well as two smaller loops at the other end. These are fastened to the cord with a → **prusik knot**. The ascent works best if you also use a carabiner on your lap belt to fasten yourself to the rope and thread the two cords through it. You can put pressure on one foot and thereby relieve the other. This opens the prusik on that side and it can be edged further upward. Now put the pressure here and open the other, and so on, until you have reached the top.

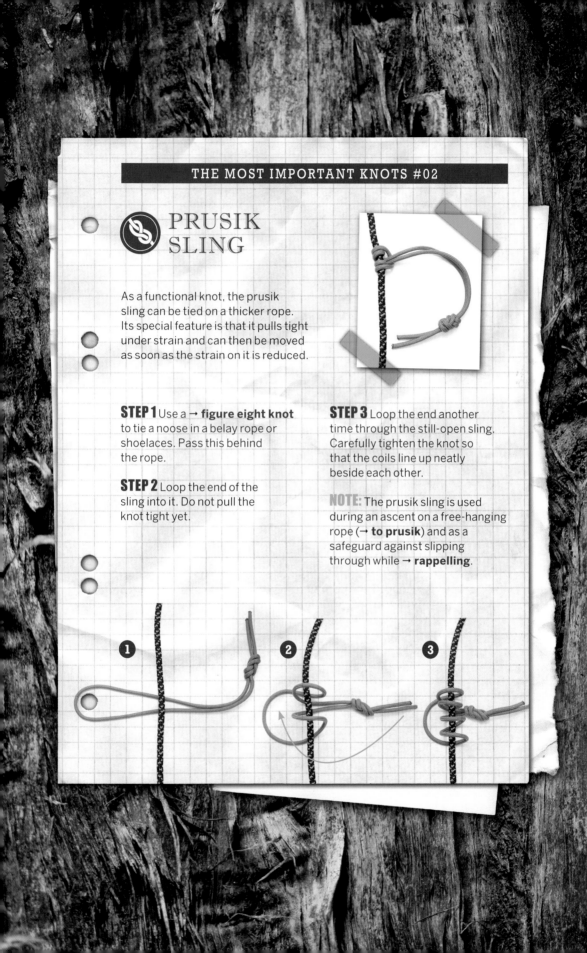

PRUSIK SLING

As a functional knot, the prusik sling can be tied on a thicker rope. Its special feature is that it pulls tight under strain and can then be moved as soon as the strain on it is reduced.

STEP 1 Use a → **figure eight knot** to tie a noose in a belay rope or shoelaces. Pass this behind the rope.

STEP 2 Loop the end of the sling into it. Do not pull the knot tight yet.

STEP 3 Loop the end another time through the still-open sling. Carefully tighten the knot so that the coils line up neatly beside each other.

NOTE: The prusik sling is used during an ascent on a free-hanging rope (→ **to prusik**) and as a safeguard against slipping through while → **rappelling**.

❶   ❷   ❸

M 6 DEALING WITH ALTITUDE SICKNESS

The air composition at higher altitudes is no different than at sea level, but the number of particles in a given volume of air is lower. To inhale the same amount of oxygen particles into your lungs, you have to breathe twice as often at half the pressure (at about 3.4 miles [5,500 m.]). The lower concentration of oxygen particles also causes reduced "exchange pressure" during diffusion. The lower amount of oxygen is also thus not absorbed into the blood when you breathe, so the blood vessels constrict and blood pressure rises. In contrast, the carbon dioxide stored in the blood is expelled particularly well, which then affects the respiratory regulation of the brain.

Even at relatively "low" altitudes (from about 1¼ miles [2,000 m.]), people who are not "altitude adjusted" can have blackouts.

General signs of altitude sickness are hyperventilation, high pulse, loss of appetite, poor circulation, and sometimes very severe headaches and insomnia.

The higher you climb (but starting at about 1.86 miles [3,000 m.]), the greater the risk of life-threatening edema, an accumulation of fluid in the brain and lungs caused by very high pressure in the blood vessels. Furthermore, the danger of → **frostbite** and general hypothermia increases due to hypoperfusion of the extremities.

Altitude acclimatization is important on high-altitude journeys. The rule applied is, "Climb high—sleep low." You should take your hours of rest at night at lower altitudes than for your daytime activities.

You can be especially seriously and noticeably affected by altitude sickness after a rapid ascent. In South America, drinking *mate de coca* or "chewing" coca leaf is an aid against the effects of high altitude. The ingredients improve the oxygenation of the body. In this form consuming the plant is actually harmless and not addictive. Outside of South America taking coca along is of course not recommended. Here → **forced air expulsion breathing** can help.

Due to the increased respiratory rate and the usually very dry mountain air the body loses a lot of fluid. You must put special emphasis on deliberately increasing your water intake.

If you have a very severe headache or your consciousness becomes clouded, the only thing that helps is descending to lower altitudes.

K14 HOW TO SURVIVE A LIGHTNING STRIKE

Besides earthquakes and volcanoes, severe weather is an elemental force that is impossible to control. While you are rarely likely to encounter seismic hazards or others in a city, lightning can strike any outdoorsman.

The ground and clouds are electrically charged during rainfall. This is compensated for by a flash of lightning, which makes the air conductive to electricity for a short time. It is hard to predict where lightning will strike, but you should take note of some protected zones and rules for what to do.

Next to the direct impact, a serious danger is posed by so-called bottom currents, when the electric current seeks a way into the earth and thus is "distributed" over the ground. Practically no human being can survive a direct lightning strike. I once found myself in such a situation along with a travel companion in the Andes. At one level a storm gathered around us—without us having any possibility for escape. To survive such an intense storm the right behavior can help; in an open area, it is often just luck.

RULES

1. Lightning usually strikes the highest elevation. Therefore, swimming and mountain climbing are especially dangerous during thunderstorms.

2. A thunderclap moves at about 1,082 fps. (330 mps.). This is roughly half a mile (a kilometer) in three seconds. Count the seconds between lightning and thunder and divide this number by three; this gives you the distance in miles (km.).

3. On the ocean or a lake, if you can no longer get to shore, you should lie down as flat as possible in your boat. If the boat has an enclosed cabin this is the safest place—even if it is raised. Similar to a car, the cabin acts as a Faraday cage—the lightning is diverted.

4. In an open field you should climb on a rock, a camping mat, or something similar and squat down without leaning on your hands. It is important that you hold your legs tightly together, otherwise ground currents could pass through your body. **Under no circumstances should you lie down during a thunderstorm!** The closer together your contact points to the ground are the lower the so-called step voltage is.

DOs AND DON'Ts IN A THUNDERSTORM

5. Stay away from trees which stand alone or ones that are particularly tall. Here, the electric shock is less of (but also) a danger than falling wreckage should the tree be hit.

6. Rocks, masts, and the like which are at least thirteen to sixteen feet (four to five meters) high form a protective cone at an angle of about 45°. However, you should not stay in the immediate vicinity due to the risk of a lightning jump.

7. And even if the proverb says otherwise, the chance of dying from a lightning strike is much more common than that of winning a million dollars in the lottery.

A storm front approaches on land flat as a pancake. Life threatening in 3 . . . 2 . . . 1.
▼

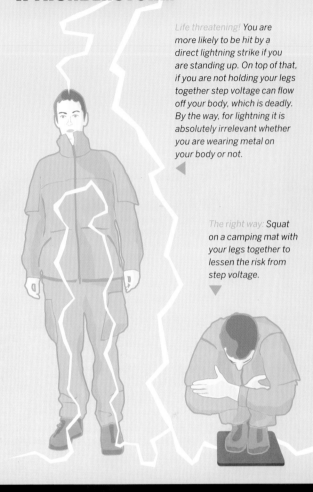

Life threatening! You are more likely to be hit by a direct lightning strike if you are standing up. On top of that, if you are not holding your legs together step voltage can flow off your body, which is deadly. By the way, for lightning it is absolutely irrelevant whether you are wearing metal on your body or not.
◄

The right way: Squat on a camping mat with your legs together to lessen the risk from step voltage.
▼

MONKEY'S FIST

You can use a round monkey's fist knot to improvise a secure anchor on rocks if you do not have a hook. Clamp the monkey's fist into a rock crevice and use it for rappelling.

STEP 1 Wind a thin rope or a belay rope three times around your finger. The rope sections must lie neatly next to each other.

STEP 2 Now in turn wind the remaining end of the rope three times around the coils, but do not wind around the knot too tightly.

STEP 3 Carefully remove the whole knot from your hand. The knot now consists of two triple loops from Step 1 and an axis from Step 2. Now thread the rope end another three times on the axis through these openings.

STEP 4 Now tighten the coils, starting from the beginning, up to the remaining end. Use a → **figure eight knot** to knot on the loop for the safety carabiner (!).

ATTENTION: When rappelling, never let a rope rub against another rope!

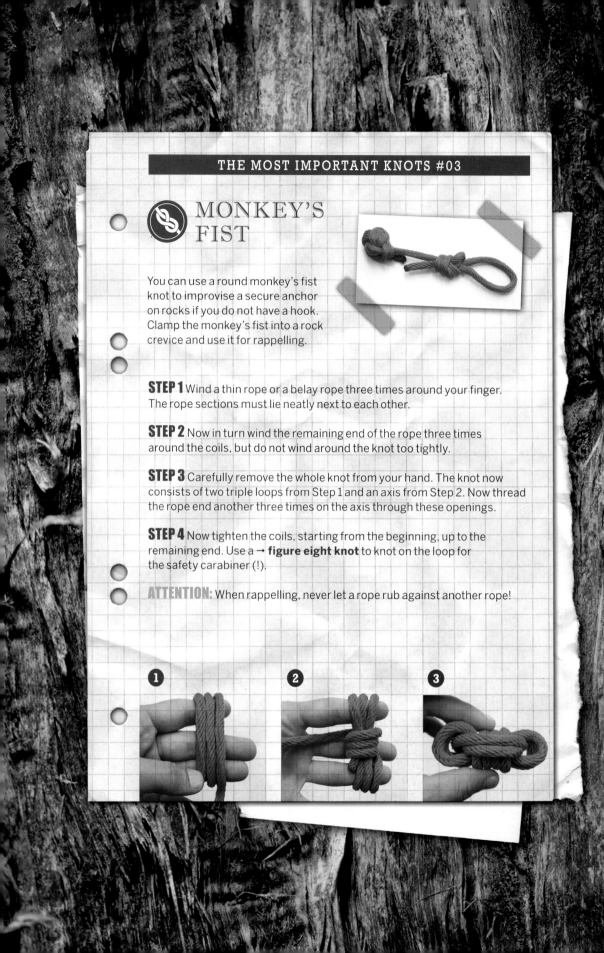

R12 DANDELION: EDIBLE BLOWBALLS

A dandelion, or what we think of as a dandelion, is in fact a number of different plants. Its certain and common distinctive feature are the showy white or butter yellow to orange composite flowers. The blossoms usually grow individually on a hollow stem, separately from the leaf rosette on the ground. The leaves are usually deeply serrated. After the blossoms fade, the parachutes of the tiny nut fruits all stand together on the head, known as a "puffball." Dandelion species have a white, milky sap. Dandelion seeds are so tiny it is only worthwhile to gather them if you have a few hundred of these heads available.

To separate them from the parachutes, first moisten the seeds and place them on a hot stone. Here the little hairs dry out, stick, and burn away. If you try to burn them off without moistening you will lose many seeds due to the heat.

It is easy to harvest large quantities of the carrot-like white roots. Some of them taste very bitter, so like → **acorns**, they must be leached in water before you eat them.

You can recognize dandelions surely and quickly by their buttery yellow flowers and typical puffball. The root is soft, but often very bitter.

K15 WHAT TO DO WHEN YOU SLIDE DOWN A HILLSIDE

Ideally, you should try to traverse mountainous regions so you avoid large ascents or descents. You can use → **contours** to find an appropriate route through difficult terrain. Nevertheless, you might have to surmount an area by crossing steep slopes. Generally, you should always try to secure yourself as much as possible. If you still slide down, you should immediately use all your body force to spread your legs out to prevent somersaulting. If you fall on your back, you should try to get into a prone position when sliding. If possible, try to press your arms as if doing a pushup against the ground to slow down in the rubble. If there is snow, try to use your hands like shovels to brake yourself.

If you fall, always try to get into a prone position.

M7 SURVIVING HIGH-ALTITUDE SUNSHINE

The air layers of our atmosphere filter out a large amount of hostile UV radiation. The higher you are traveling, the more you have to pay attention to sun protection, especially in the equatorial mountains.

Even if the sky is overcast, you can get severe sunburns from UV radiation and eye damage from the glaring light in less than one hour. You must apply sunscreen (SPF 60+) to every exposed part of your body. You should at least cover the larger body areas with UV protective clothing.

Balaclavas and glacier glasses are essential in places where there is lots of reflection (from ice, snow, and water).

GLACIER GLASSES → page 100

IMPROVISED SNOW GOGGLES → page 104

NATURAL SUN PROTECTION → page 205

M8 MAKE SPLINTS FOR A BROKEN LEG

If a larger bone, such as the lower leg, is broken during a fall, the leg should be stretched and splinted for transporting the patient out, so that the sharp edges of bone do not damage muscle tissue or blood vessels.

STEP 1 Cut a long forked branch so that when it is attached at the hip the branch still protrudes well below the foot.

STEP 2 Tie a loop over the foot and stretch it over the branch end. When doing this apply heavy traction to the foot—the shortened muscles need to be re-stretched.

STEP 3 Fasten the rope and tie the leg to the branch with many loops.

Thus stabilized, the injured person can be transported safely.

ATTENTION: You should not try to stabilize any break of a thigh or hip—a wrong move could cause life-threatening internal hemorrhage.

K16 IMPROVISE A LAP BELT

If you find that you unexpectedly have to rappel or secure yourself somewhere and have at least one carabiner and a stable rope (with a static rope you can only secure yourself on a slope with a very small drop height, no lead climb security, etc.), you can enhance your safety with an improvised lap belt. But you should **never plan to use such a belt** when mountaineering. First make a large loop with rope using a → **figure eight knot**. Always put the loop behind you. Using both hands, guide the side of the loop around your hips and pull the lower part between your legs. Everything is held together in front with the carabiner.

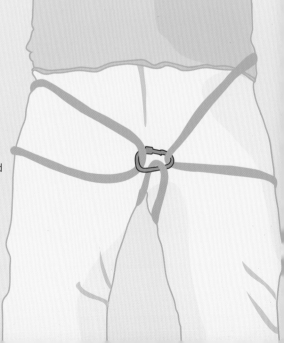

GARDA HITCH

When you want to lift a heavy load—such as a hunted animal to field dress it—but it keeps sliding down, a blocking device such as a garda hitch is a big help.

STEP 1 Hook two carabiners into a loop at the end of a rope or in a quickdraw from climbing. It is important that the openings face the same direction.

STEP 2 Suspend the rope to be used for lifting or pulling the load from both carabiners. The end where the load will be attached is thus on the rear side.

STEP 3 Now thread the rope in front again through the upper carabiner. If you pull on the front end the rope slips through the garda hitch; if you let go, the rope will be blocked and will not drop back again.

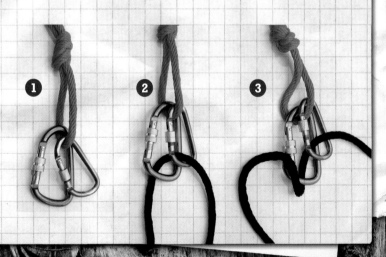

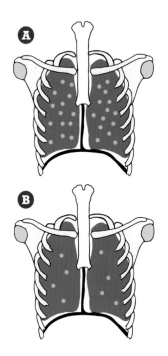

M9 THIN AIR—FORCED AIR EXPULSION

A special breathing technique can temporarily help altitude sickness. **Forced air expulsion means that, after inhaling, the lungs are first pressed by contracting the chest before the air is slowly exhaled.** You can also exhale by hissing through your teeth, "trumpeting," or humming as you breathe out. The effect is the same. For example, if you are carrying a heavy load during an ascent you have to take control so as not to hyperventilate. Compressing the lungs during forced air expulsion slightly decreases lung volume, in turn providing more oxygen particles per unit volume in the lungs. This facilitates their diffusion.

◀

At sea level **A**, *there are significantly more oxygen particles* ● *per lung volume than in air at high altitudes* **B**.

M10 RELOCATE A DISLOCATED SHOULDER

Dislocating a shoulder is one of the most common larger limb injuries. A light fall, when you instinctively catch yourself by the arms, can quickly dislocate a shoulder. The upper arm is held very loosely in the shallow *glenoid fossa* by ligaments and muscles. If you fall in the mountains, it is relatively likely you could dislocate this joint. Besides a light rolling fall on to your outstretched arm or shoulder, just clasping tightly to a rock if you are sliding can be enough to pry the shoulder joint from its anchorage. Generally these dislocations are brief, and after a frightening moment the bone jumps back in to the joint. But if the joint is fully dislocated it must be treated as soon as possible, since the overstretched ligaments and muscles will contract rapidly, and after that relocation can only be done surgically. Afterward, the arm should be splinted and stabilized.

WHAT TO DO TO RELOCATE:
Press the back of the injured person against a tree or rock while standing or sitting (1) and push the elbow against the body under tension (2), then lever it, under tension, in a forward-upward rotation (3). The joint should slip back into its correct place with a snapping noise. Then use a shawl or a rope to bind a support strap to relieve pressure on the arm.

▶

The combination of movements to relocate a shoulder.

▲
Get your bearings on the horizon with your arm outstretched and count fingers up to the sun.

K17 DETERMINE YOUR REMAINING DAYLIGHT

In the mountains, it is especially important to be capable of quickly estimating residual daytime so you can descend in time or seek a safe place in daylight using the hand method. It is relatively inaccurate, but enough to get a rough estimate.

With your hand outstretched, count the number of fingers the sun still stands above the horizon. Three to five fingers correspond to about one hour, depending on season and location. It is not possible to figure out the actual time more precisely because things vary too much by season and location.

W6 WATER REQUIREMENTS AT HIGH ALTITUDES

If you are mountaineering at altitudes above 3,280 ft. (1,000 m.), your demand for water rises rapidly. At 1.86 miles (3,000 m.) above sea level, you need about twice as much water as at sea level. The reason for this is the reduced oxygen content in the blood makes your blood pressure rise and all the organs do not function normally. Depending on your fighting weight, you should reckon on needing approximately the following additional amount of water:

Body weight	Additional water per 3,280 ft. (1,000 m.) altitude
up to 110 lbs.	17 oz.
110–176 lbs.	23.7 oz.
176–220 lbs.	27 oz.
over 220 lbs.	34 oz.

Few living creatures have adapted to a permanent existence in eternal ice. Man has to face sub-zero temperatures essentially naked. The major challenge is withstanding snowstorms and the night, when it is impossible to move. The body cools down very quickly and loses enormous amounts of energy.

SURVIVAL IN THE ICE+SNOW

Outer Space

The falling snow dampens any sound. The noise of the frozen snow breaking under my lined boots penetrates my ears as if through cotton.

Frozen nature survives the winter by waiting and resting; one strategy I know I will not put into effect. In a short time, people can lose this unequal struggle forever. Perhaps that is the reason why mankind has tried to use every physical and technical possibility to defy this climate. Nevertheless, it is clear that, at most, we only have visiting rights in this demanding region.

E13 EQUIPMENT FOR ICY COLD

In many climatic regions you can find enough building material, such as wood, leaves, or plant fibers, to protect yourself from bad or cold weather, but when temperatures fall below zero, it is barely possible to survive through the night.

The serious dangers posed by ice, wet snow, and avalanches make some kinds of equipment irreplaceable for training.

Regions that combine icy cold with the adversities posed by high altitudes are particularly dangerous.

Down jacket: In dry cold, the thick padding of down garments is just sufficient to prevent hypothermia over a longer time.

Life saver: Two tent pegs tied together through your sleeves make a rescue tool if the ice breaks.

Mittens: Since fingertips freeze more easily in gloves with individual fingers you need mittens, or gloves with at least two fingers together.

Thermos: If you carry a thermos, you can always have a warm drink along the way.

Avalanche probe: To search for buried people.

Avalanche transceiver: Carrying an avalanche transceiver is particularly important in hilly regions.

Down shoes: When bivouacking in snow your toes often freeze first. Down shoe liners protect against this.

Snow shovel: A tool to remove or excavate snow.

K18 AVALANCHE SURVIVAL

Every year many people die in avalanches. To be able to assess the risk, you should take a special avalanche course at a climbing club or generally avoid avalanche risk areas. It is difficult to assess whether and where an avalanche will occur, especially if you do not know the weather conditions during past days. **In areas at risk, you should carry an avalanche transceiver (Digital Transceiver System, or DTS) with you.** After an avalanche falls a person can survive in the snow fifteen to thirty minutes. You are rarely buried more than 3¼ feet deep, but the snow is so firmly compacted you cannot dig yourself out.

If you get caught in an avalanche, you can increase your chances of survival by doing the following:

>> Discard everything that hinders your ability to move: backpack, skis, hiking poles, etc.

>> Observe where your companions are so you can help them in case of an avalanche. If possible, make an emergency call immediately.

>> If you have an avalanche transceiver try to narrow down the avalanche site as quickly as possible.

>> If you do not have a transceiver, try to find a thin branch, tent rod, or an avalanche probe as fast as possible to probe for victims.

NOTE: In areas which are at risk, you can take along a loosely coiled paracord with an inflated condom or something comparable knotted on. Tie the other end to your belt. Release the cord and balloon during an avalanche. The buoyant balloon will float to the surface and can point rescuers to your location by lying on the snow.

Aid devices such as a DTS, avalung, avalanche ball, or avalanche airbag certainly increase your likelihood of survival, **but do not provide any security against being killed by an avalanche**. You can only rule out getting caught in an avalanche by avoiding at-risk regions.

>> If you find someone buried, dig them out as carefully and as quickly as possible. If the person is not breathing perform → **resuscitation** immediately. If → **hypothermic**, they must be warmed up correctly.

>> If you cannot find the person buried, try to mark the place they were caught by the avalanche and the point they went under as accurately as possible for any rescue team which might arrive in time to rescue them.

>> Try to keep yourself on the surface of the avalanche by using swimming motions, kicking and jumping.

>> If you are pulled under the snow, immediately use your hands to form a hollow space around your mouth. Many avalanche victims die by suffocation in the snow in and in front of their mouths.

>> If you hear steps or voices scream for your life.

If you were not caught by the avalanche you should help your companions.

Use an avalanche probe to systematically examine the area you assume avalanche victims are.

◀

R13 ACORN ENERGY BARS

In northern latitudes it can be very difficult to find food under a blanket of snow. If you look for wooded areas and find some gnarled oaks you will have enough to eat. Heaps of acorns, which drop from the tree in autumn, lie under the blanket of snow, well chilled and therefore still edible, even in late winter. After → **leaching out the tannins** you can make → **pemmican-like** energy bars. Grind the chopped and leached acorns **(1)** to a pulp, adding gathered insects and berries, and spread the entirety on a wooden board. First dry the bar by the fire **(2)** and then roast it; you can take it along as a starchy and oil-rich emergency food that lasts a long time.

W7 SNOW = DRINKING WATER?

Very often the question arises whether you can drink snow or glacier water directly. Apart from the high heat needed to melt it there is nothing wrong with this. Like any precipitation, snow and glacier water which has accumulated over centuries are virtually sterile. Mineral content is very low compared to "drinking water" from a bottle and corresponds to distilled water.

The human body can process very large amounts of distilled water without difficulty. It is problematic to drink distilled water in very hot climates (→ **hyperhydration**), where the amount of normal drinking water which can cause water intoxication is not much larger.

In an environment where you do not sweat excessively it is not a problem to drink mineral-poor glacial water.

You can drink melted water from snow or ice without hesitation in cold regions.
▼

R14 AUTOMATIC FISHING IN AN ICE HOLE

Ice fishing is a very good option on a totally frozen and snow-covered sheet of ice. Fish like to gather under holes where light penetrates. Use a hatchet to punch a hole and skim away the ice floating on the water. Now bind two pieces of wood crossways to each other and tie a baited fishing line to one end. Place the cross on the ice so it can be drawn halfway into the hole when a fish is hanging on it. This gives you a bite indicator so you can fish through several holes from the shore.

◀

If a fish bites, the cross stands up in the hole and shows you have a bite.

S5 SNOW CAVES— EMERGENCY BIVOUAC

You can dig a snow cave quickly for an emergency bivouac. Cover the entrance so it does not let in a draft.

▼

Even in an emergency you should avoid bivouacking at night, outside the forest or at least the hills. There you are at the mercy of an icy storm and can become cold very quickly. To survive such a situation overnight you can build a snow cave to bivouac.

Dig up a layer of snow from an area about 3.28×6.5 ft. (1×2 m.) wide and loosen it. Remove the snow as deep as possible using eating utensils or a shovel. At a depth of about three feet dig a recess into the wall on the long side to make a sleeping place about sixteen to twenty-four inches (forty to sixty cm.) high, three feet wide, and slightly longer than your height. Insulate the bottom of this small chamber from the snow by using as much cushioning material as you can.

If you are wearing warm winter clothes you can spend the night in a snow cave without a problem. If the draft is too strong you can narrow the entry with snow shingles or cover it with a jacket, but you must make sure you have a sufficient air supply.

E14 OPTIMIZE YOUR GLACIER GLASSES

In very bright and low sunlight reflecting on water, ice, or snow, the light penetrating your glacier glasses may be too strong, despite the highest level of darkening.

To prevent snow blindness, you can cover the glass with a little tape. This will cover the very bright areas, such as ground or sky.

If you wear prescription glasses you can use this method to improvise snow goggles by taping over the glasses, leaving only a very narrow gap.

When the sun is low on the horizon and blinds you, tape can be a quick solution.

W8 MELT SNOW INTO DRINKING WATER

If you are traveling in low temperatures it is not easy to come by liquid water. Lakes and rivers are frozen over, and a huge effort is needed to get water.

Although water is available in frozen form, it takes a lot of energy to convert it to a liquid state. **If you suck on snow balls you lose large amounts of energy that you have to recover by eating food.**

You can melt snow by simply impaling a compact clump of snow on a stick of wood and setting it over a pot by the fire. As it warms water drips into the pot.

This method, compared to melting snow in a pot on the fire, has the advantage that you do not have to use an additional small fire to cook; you can do it right by your warming fire. Snow also has a much bigger volume than water, so you would have to keep filling the

pot. Using skewers, you can easily melt several times the volume of a pot or cup and do not have to constantly worry about it.

M11 EVALUATE FROSTBITE

Frostbite affecting complete parts of the body does not happen from one moment to the next, but is usually the result of persistent dehydration and hypoperfusion during a summit storm lasting several hours, or an unplanned emergency bivouac in the snow. Here the primary thing is to minimize the risk of → **hypothermia**, and only after you can sustain body heat should you deal with any possible frostbite.

Superficial frostbite of the skin may develop relatively quickly if you are wearing the wrong clothes in strong winds, but it is usually not too serious. Exposed body parts such as noses and ears freeze especially quickly.

The level of injury is practically the same as from a burn; you usually cannot see frostbite right away, since you cannot take off your clothes until hours or days after suffering the hypothermia which caused it when you reach a warm environment.

1ST DEGREE Under-circulation in bluish-pale skin, pain, and swelling.

2ND DEGREE Bluish-red patches of skin with blistering.

3RD DEGREE The skin and underlying tissue mortify without pain.

4TH DEGREE Part of the body is completely frozen. Ice crystals are formed as the water component in tissues solidify, irreversibly destroying all the surrounding cells. **If a body part is already frozen solid it can no longer be saved.**

You can only warm up frostbite if you can rule out that you will be exposed to severe cold again. In cold regions this is usually the case only after the descent, or you reach civilization.

Various complications, such as thrombosis or infection, may occur. In no case should you rub or massage any body part still in the frozen state or after it thaws out, since this can cause further mechanical injuries and more tissue death.

After *slowly* thawing in warm water or by a heat source—which may only be done if you can treat a general hypothermia by warming up the torso, or can rule it out —the dead black and blue tissue will peel off the still-living parts and dry out. *It takes months to be able to estimate if and how much of a limb must be removed.*

Frostbite kills and discolors skin and muscle cells. If your fingers look like this you should see a doctor.

▼

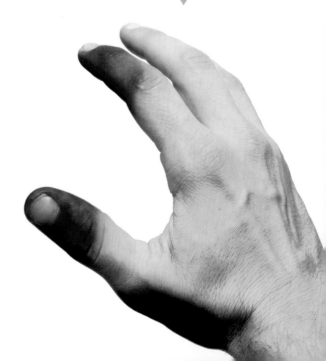

ATTENTION: It is impossible to fully treat severe frostbite outdoors.

A whiteout can cause
serious difficulties for
people traveling in the
Arctic and mountaineers,
because you cannot
assess heights. A
seemingly small jump
can land you several
hundred feet down.

K19 WHITEOUT—LOSS OF CONTRAST

When you have bright ground, overcast sky, snow or fog, and strong sunlight at the same time, the environment can be "overexposed" to the human eye, so that you can no longer recognize contours such as natural features, precipices, or slopes. Visibility is often severely limited—you can barely estimate distances and heights.

Travelers often keep trying to go forward in such a situation (for example, with a small window of time to reach a summit)—often with a fatal outcome.

Since navigating with a map and compass is hardly possible you can follow a GPS tracker, but this is generally not recommended. **To keep moving forward during a whiteout can endanger your life. Crevasses, precipices, and obstacles can become deadly traps.** The only correct response is to look for a safe place in the immediate vicinity and rest or bivouac in a snow cave or in an igloo—if necessary for several days.

You can find rushes even in the winter, because the stalks grow up to six and a half feet tall. The rhizomes can be eaten raw or cooked.

R15 RUSHES AS EMERGENCY RATIONS

Rushes or reeds are a common grass which grows all over the world and are mainly found in large fields by bodies of water. The upright stems are studded with oblong leaves, as also seen on small grasses. Depending on the subspecies, the plants are up to thirty feet tall and a few inches thick. Atop the field of reeds reddish to gray flowers bloom **(1)**, and bushy spikelets together form foxtails **(2)**. The whitish rhizomes **(3)** creep underground; you can dig these up with a little effort. In the spring, you can pull the bright green tops from the stalk and eat them like palm hearts. There is only one kind of reed worldwide, with several subspecies; the plants differ only in size and color. The reed is one of the plants you can find in winter in a few feet of snow. Here reeds, together with → **cattails**, are one of the few available sources of food. Ground close to water is often only superficially frozen, which can make digging easier.

E15 IMPROVISE SNOW GOGGLES

When the ground is very bright make the slits as small as possible.

The sun's reflection shining through snow and ice can cause eye strain, which can lead to inflammation and temporary blindness.

You can improvise snow goggles using any fabric you have with you. Cut two small slits in a strip of cloth as far apart as your eyes. You can also improvise snow goggles with tape and your prescription glasses.

E16 IMPROVISED SKIS

If you have enough time, you can make → **snowshoes** for walking along the trap line. If you have to move in ice and snow rapidly skis are often more suitable than snowshoes.

You can make improvised skis with the aid of a normal woodcarving knife. Look out for a young hazel, pine, or maple trunk about two to three inches in diameter.

Split it using a → **wedge** or knife and flatten it on both sides using the → **power cut**.

Make the underside of the ski somewhat rounded—this makes such skis unsuitable for carving, but they are for use as cross-country skis on deep snow, because this increases the contact surface. When skiing, the tips do not dig into the snow and you move forward fluidly. They are tapered forward and → **bowed over a fire**. You can maintain the curvature by using a cord to stretch the tip taut over a support. Make notches in the middle of the ski for tying on your shoes. You can seal the cords that go over the running surface with → **resin adhesive**.

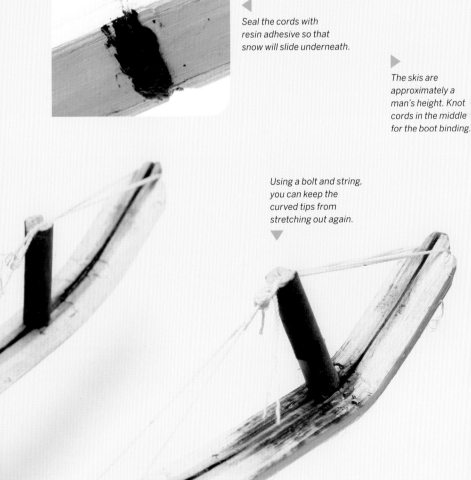

Seal the cords with resin adhesive so that snow will slide underneath.

The skis are approximately a man's height. Knot cords in the middle for the boot binding.

Using a bolt and string, you can keep the curved tips from stretching out again.

F6 FIRE ON ICE

Fire is hot and ice melts in heat. A campfire can frequently sink into wet snow after a short time. How can you still build a campfire in deep winter snow or on a frozen lake to grill the fish you caught, or to thaw out your shoes after a bitterly cold night?

In winter, natives of cold regions make their campfires on a wooden platform. Wood insulates well against the heat of the fire and protects the ice beneath from melting.

If possible, coat the simple platform with mud or earth. The heat seals the wood with a fire resistant layer and prevents the platform from burning.

A simple wooden platform prevents the campfire from sinking down. ▼

K20 ESCAPING FROM THIN ICE

When traveling in ice and snow, you will sometimes have to cross frozen bodies of water, whether you want to or not. Due to the flowing water, you can never predict whether the ice is thick enough, and it can also become brittle in some places. As a result, there is a danger of falling through into freezing water. This is **life-threatening**. Within three to four minutes you can lose consciousness. When crossing ice, you should always carry two pegs secured by a cord. This gives you a tool you can use if the ice breaks to pull yourself over the mirror-smooth surface and out of the water.

To get quickly back on land, draw up one leg and use it to lift yourself up to the edge of the hole. At the same time fix the pegs into the ice and use them to pull yourself out. It is best to slide to the shore on your stomach to prevent the ice from breaking again.

Tent pegs can be lifesavers if you fall through the ice. ▶

✦ ORIENTATION BY THE SUN

If you want to move forward without a compass in an area with no distinctly visible terrain features, you can easily and fairly accurately determine the four cardinal directions by the sun.

To do this, insert a rod vertically into ground that is as flat as possible. Mark the end of the shadow cast by the stick. A quarter hour later the shadow will have moved. Again mark the end of the shadow. The connecting line indicates east-west precisely enough. The longer you wait, the more accurate the direction indicator is.

The last shadow cast always marks the eastern end, whether you are in the southern or northern hemisphere. With a rough knowledge of the four compass directions you can approximate your desired direction of march by bisecting the angle.

To determine the direction as precisely as possible you should do your sun orientation shortly before and shortly after 12 o'clock. ▶

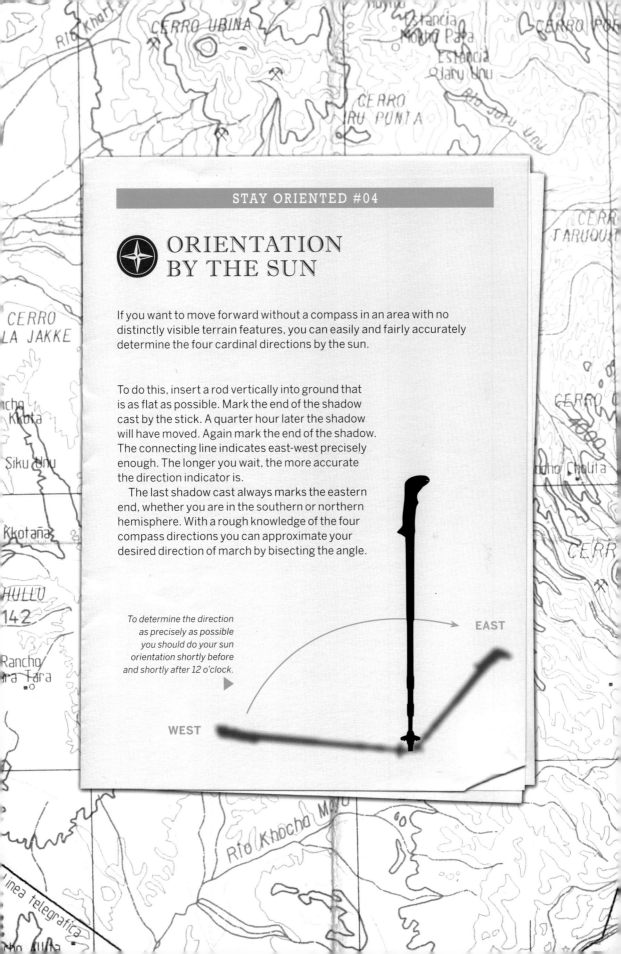

EAST

WEST

M12 HYPOTHERMIA

Freezing is one of the leading causes of death for extreme travelers and mountaineers, expedition paddlers, and Arctic travelers.

While humans have an insulating layer of fat under the skin, this is not always enough to prevent heat loss. You lose your mental capacities particularly quickly if the brain can no longer maintain its working temperature—which can happen shockingly fast.

If you fall into ice-cold water you have a few minutes of reaction time, then you will become unconscious. Ten minutes later you will be dead.

Cold damp weather, strong winds, and high altitudes can also greatly speed up freezing (so-called wind chill).

The process of freezing is divided into different stages, depending on residual body temperature. Treatment in each case is by warming, and differs depending on the condition of the patient.

The first measure is always to get the casualty out of their immediate emergency situation, that is, rescue them from the water or snow cave.

ATTENTION: Rewarming must always be done starting from the torso—never on the extremities, or even using a warm bath.

If the patient recovers consciousness as they warm up, take particular care to ensure they are kept lying still, even if they want to move, and that the torso is warmed up externally or with warm drinks.

1. LIGHT HYPOTHERMIA

(core temperature 98.6–95°F [37–35°C]):
Symptoms: Strong sensitivity to cold, shivering, shaking, but *fully conscious*.
Treatment: Active physical exercise, such as running, straight jumps, etc., to raise muscle temperature. Drink warm fluids, warm up by the fire.

2. MODERATE HYPOTHERMIA

(core temperature 95–89.6°F [35–32°C]):
Symptoms: Severe shaking, rapid pulse and breathing, reduced judgment capacity, *incipient hypoperfusion of the extremities* (the blood is colder here than in the torso!).
Treatment: Active movement, and additional thermal insulation using dry clothes, a sleeping bag, or an emergency blanket. Otherwise, as for 1.

3. INTERMEDIATE HYPOTHERMIA

(core temperature 89.6–82.4°F [32–28°C]):
Symptoms: Sharply reduced level of consciousness, extreme fatigue and tiredness, reduced shaking, slowed pulse, and shallow breathing.
Treatment: Carefully remove wet clothing without any sudden movement (danger of perforation because the blood is very cold in the arms and legs). Lay the patient down carefully on a camping mat, provide heat insulation with an emergency blanket, and over it dry clothes, a sleeping bag, etc.

4. SEVERE HYPOTHERMIA:

(core temperature below 82.4°F [28°C]):
Symptoms: Deep unconsciousness, circulatory arrest, respiratory arrest, and death. It is very difficult to warm up and save anyone with a core temperature below 82.4°F [28°C] without intensive medical treatment just with normal travel equipment.
Treatment: Insulation, and do not move the patient! In case of circulatory arrest apply immediate resuscitation. Warm them up very slowly by placing hot water bottles on the abdomen.

THE SHEET BEND

If you want to extend a rope using a thinner line, you need a special knot. This is useful for lengthening tow ropes or guy ropes. It is important to make sure that the correct knot is tied in the thinner or thicker rope.

STEP 1 Double back the thick rope. Pass the thin rope through the resulting bight from underneath. Make sure you do the steps in this sequence.

STEP 2 Wind the thin rope from inside to outside around the short end of the loop in the thick rope. Position the short end of the thin rope behind both ends of the thick rope.

STEP 3 Now draw the cord over the bight, and as you do so, thread it under the long end coming out of the bight. Tighten the knot by holding the thick rope at both ends and the thin rope is slid on to the end of the loop.

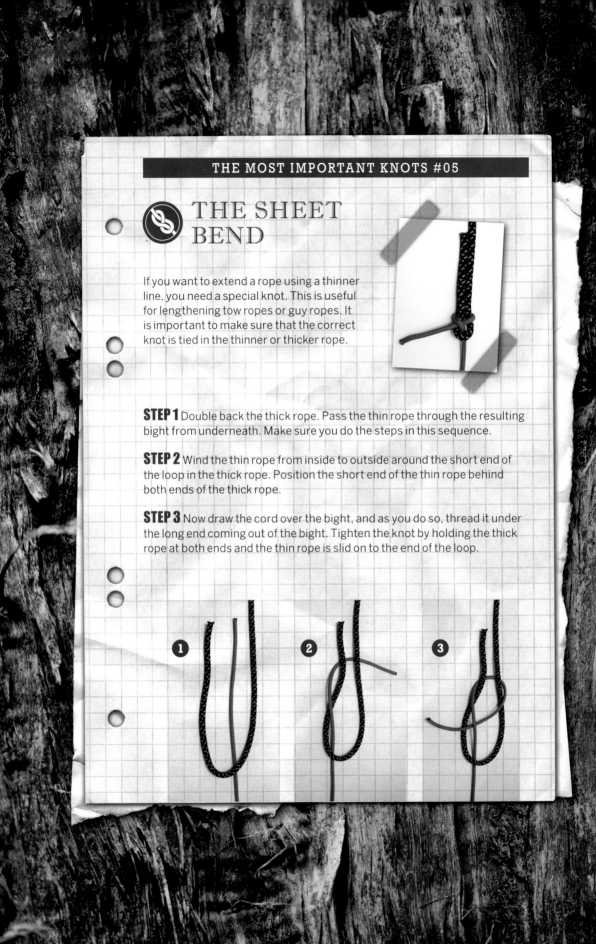

S6 BUILD AN IGLOO

If you want to spend a longer time in one place and do not want to just bivouac, you can build a bigger igloo. Without practice and knowledge of how the snow must be constituted, it makes no sense to cut snow blocks and to stack them on each other.

The simpler method is to gather a large pile of loose snow. Push a couple sticks about six to eight inches (15–20 cm.) long into the snow to mark the wall thickness for later. On the downwind side have the snow pile taper off somewhat. Now use your eating utensils to dig into the pile from this side until you reach the markers or pole tips. If there is enough snow, you can also construct a cold trap as an entryway (cold air from outside sinks and remains in the depression). Such an igloo is considerably warmer than a simple bivouac cave and can even be heated, as long as you make sure it is ventilated.

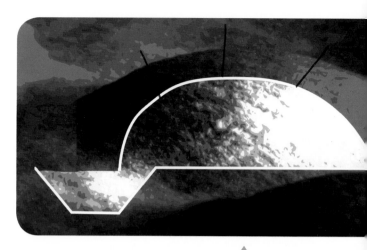

You can dig a simple igloo into a pile of snow. This is faster than sawing blocks of snow.

E17 IMPROVISE SNOWSHOES

Snowshoes made from a wooden frame and cord work better than twigs tied together.

Your feet sink quickly into deep snow; even on frozen snow you break through the surface and can hardly move from a spot. Snowshoes or improvised → **skis** can make all the difference. Of course, you can easily bind a few pine branches under your feet.

But if you are going a longer way, the right snowshoes are a real advantage. You can make them from a thick forked stick that you mortise at the lower end with a crossbar, like a → **makeshift saw**. String this frame with cloth or → **leather**, or fasten a net into it. Suitable knots for making the net are the → **lark's head knot** and → **square knot**. First make a lot of loops on one side. When you come to the end, knot two loops at a time using the lark's head or square knot. This creates a new row of loops. When you reach the end, tie the knots in the opposite direction until the entire snowshoe is filled with a sturdy net.

NOTE: Traditionally, the net is knotted from bands of damp rawhide. These contract as they dry, strongly tightening up the entire net and stabilizing the mortise.

Water is life. This element, so strange to us, covers most of our planet. It offers food and the possibility of transport and cooling off. But it also poses great dangers. Many thousands of people drown or become hypothermic in lakes, or are dragged under when crossing a river. An unknown number die in shipwrecks or capsize in storms. In this chapter we deal with the most important special features for survival in a wet environment.

SURVIVAL IN/ON THE WATER

The Deep Peace of Solitude

The clock has taken control of humans' daily lives. We plan our appointments to the second, and deal with our lives by dividing them into blocks and modules. Often we humans only find out how unsuited we are for this life when we slow down.

An independent life in solitude quickly makes us realize how our totally organized lives gnaw away at our physical and mental resources—and how good it is to forget this for a time, even if you do not have a pool and a Caipirinha.

If we have trained in survival techniques, this allows us to make the leap from the city into complete wilderness, to adapt to our own way of keeping time which has nothing to do with wearing a chronometer on your wrist. To be awakened not by an alarm, but by the first rays of sunshine.

Instead of rushing to a supermarket to shop and eat breakfast on the run, to gather and hunt your own food for the day. Especially to listen to your own body and to regenerate it when it holds this to be necessary.

E18 EQUIPMENT FOR IN AND ON THE WATER

It is the archetypal survival emergency; you are stranded on a desert island or floating in a lifeboat on the sea. But even if, less spectacularly, you are kayaking, there are a few pieces of equipment that should always be at hand on a boat.

In water-rich forests and plains, we often forget to take water-specific equipment along, though it may be necessary to cross a body of water on an improvised boat or rope bridge.

In coastal areas you will always seek out the sea to collect food and building materials, or emergency rations.

By the time you want to swim away from your desert island, you will find a few pieces of equipment very helpful.

▲ *Fishing reel:* Fishing line and some hooks for obtaining food.

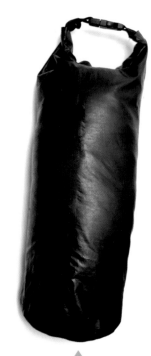

▲ *Packsack:* A waterproof sack to hold a second set of dry clothes.

Life jacket: Whether a solid life jacket or an automatic system, you should always take a flotation device along for any activities in or on the water.

▶

Flotation device with at least a thirty-three-foot-long stable line: To rescue anyone who has fallen into the water or to build a rope bridge.

Signal light: A waterproof flashlight will make you visible even at night in case of distress at sea.

▶

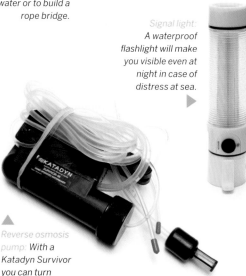

▲ *Reverse osmosis pump: With a Katadyn Survivor you can turn salt water into drinking water.*

R16 HOW TO GUT A FISH

If you have caught a fish and → **killed it humanely**, then you will have to scale and gut it before cooking or grilling. To scale it, take a knife or a sharp-edged stone and scrape the fish skin rapidly from tail to head. Be careful not to hurt yourself on the spines in the fins or behind the gills. Then slit open the fish belly from throat to cloaca. Do not cut in too deeply, so you do not cut into the intestines. After cutting it open, cut off the gullet on the head side and pull the stomach, liver, intestines, and all attached organs from the fish. If it is a freshwater fish you can also eat the liver. Some saltwater fish organs may be toxic. If the gall bladder, which is attached to the liver, bursts, this is not too much of a problem; wash out the fish as quickly as possible and that's it. After removing the organs, you still have to scrape out the dark red kidneys, which grow along the backbone. They have a slightly bitter taste. If this does not bother you you can leave them there. If the fish is to be dried or → **smoked** remove the gills, since they disintegrate rapidly.

W9 FRESHWATER LENS ON A SECLUDED BEACH

If you get into distress on a sailing trip and just barely save yourself by reaching a small island which has no water source, you will die of thirst. Right? Wrong! Even if they are just a few thousand feet in diameter, islands can sometimes store hundreds of thousands of cubic feet of potable or fresh water. This is due to a phenomenon known as the Ghyben-Herzberg lens: When it rains on the island, rainwater seeps through the sand into the ground. Islands have no natural groundwater table, but are under-washed by salt water. Because salt water is heavier than fresh water, and the rainfall only seeps through the sand slowly, a so-called freshwater lens is stored above the mean sea level. To reach it, look for the lowest possible place on the island and begin to dig there. Often you do not have to dig deep: the fresh water level is above sea level.

ATTENTION, MYTH: This phenomenon has led to the idea that sand can filter the salt out of seawater, but that does not work. You will only find water on the beach if there is an underground river flowing into the sea.

R17 HARD SHELL, SOFT CORE: WATER SNAILS

Snails do not just live on land, but also in water. Some of these are real delicacies. You should only consume snails that have shells; shell-less water snails are usually toxic. Some of them release a lovely color into the water. Marine snails with conical shells have a venomous harpoon; you should only touch them for the shortest time possible. Freshwater snails often have a brackish taste. They are better grilled than boiled.

To kill snails either place them, opening at the top, in the embers or toss them into boiling water. You can use a wooden skewer to pull the grilled snail from the shell and eat it.

All water snails with a solid shell are edible, however, they absolutely must be heated prior to consumption, because they can transmit various parasites (such as liver fluke).

K21 HOW TO SEND SIGNALS WITH A MIRRORED SURFACE

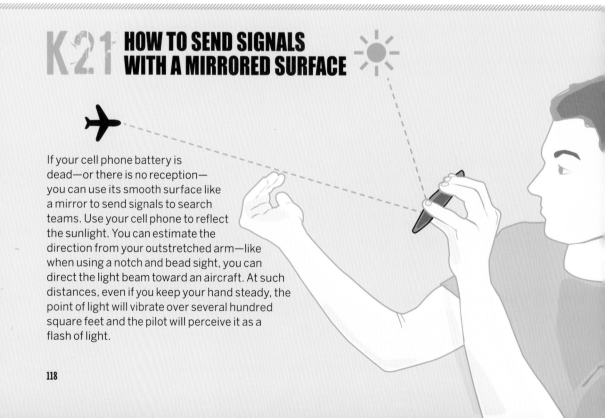

If your cell phone battery is dead—or there is no reception—you can use its smooth surface like a mirror to send signals to search teams. Use your cell phone to reflect the sunlight. You can estimate the direction from your outstretched arm—like when using a notch and bead sight, you can direct the light beam toward an aircraft. At such distances, even if you keep your hand steady, the point of light will vibrate over several hundred square feet and the pilot will perceive it as a flash of light.

FISH HOOK KNOTS

All over the world, especially in developing countries, eyeless fish hooks are used more often than those with eyelets because they are easier and cheaper to manufacture. If your → **survival kit** fish hook is broken, you should know how to knot an eyeless hook tight.

STEP 1 Hold the fishing line in a hairpin loop along the "shaft" of the hook. The excess should be at least four inches (ten centimeters) long on the shorter end.

STEP 2 Starting from the flat part, tightly wind the short end at least seven times around the "shaft" and loop. To do this you will have to keep shifting your grip.

STEP 3 When you reach the curve of the hook, thread the end through the still-projecting loop.

IMPORTANT: Keep the coils narrow and close to each other. Moisten the knot with saliva before pulling it tight.

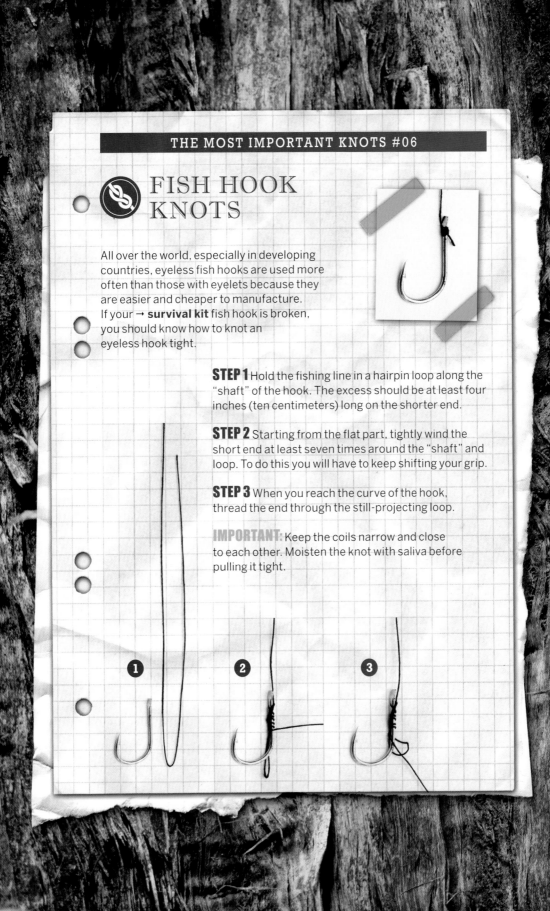

W10 CONDOM WATER DESALINATION

Anyone sailing on salt water for a longer period who does not have a → **reverse osmosis pump** will die of thirst sooner or later.

If you have a condom and a small container in your survival pack, you can make a condom distiller. Fill the container with some salt water and seal it with the condom. Inflate and knot the condom.

Hang your still up in the sun. **The heat will make the water evaporate and condense in the rubber sheath.**

After a few hours you have a shot glass of condom-tasting drinking water. Not much and not very tasty, but you know it is not harmful, and may be just the amount you need until you are rescued.

K22 A DRIFT ANCHOR FOR ROUGH SEAS

Worst case: You are out sailing on the sea in a boat in heavy weather and the engine stalls or your fuel runs out. The boat can be hard to handle, capsize, or be rolled over by breaking waves. To prevent this, you can put together a drift anchor using a tent, canvas, or the like on a rope over the bow. Leave about as much line so that the drift anchor and boat will be on the wave crest or in the trough at the same time. The boat can now align itself pointing into the waves, will no longer roll so heavily, and offers less contact surface.

To improvise a drift anchor, fasten two equally long pieces of rope crosswise to the corners of a large piece of fabric (→ sheet bend). Tie this to the anchor line (→ bowline).

R18 A CRAWLY DELICACY— CATCH AND PREPARE CRABS

You can find crustaceans in almost all the world's waters. They taste wonderful and are easy to catch. Small crustaceans include woodlice and amphipods; these can be easily collected.

Hold crabs by their hindmost legs. They can't reach behind the carapace with their pincers. **Hold crayfish** on the side of the carapace.

They sit in rivers under stones or submerged in small mud holes.

Crabs must be cooked, because they can transmit lungworm. Depending on their size, it is enough to cook crabs for five to ten minutes. After boiling, the carapace turns red.

You can eat all the soft parts in the carapace—muscles and offal.

Crayfish (left) must be grasped directly behind the pincers on the head shell. Hold crabs (right) at the end of the carapace, or by the rear pair of legs.

There are freshwater shrimp and small shrimp in rivers all over the world. It's best to catch them in a net or a leafy branch.

Before eating you have to crack the hard crab shell.

121

K23 TORRENTIAL RIVERS

If your canoe or raft capsizes in whitewater or the current pulls you off your feet, **your life is in danger**.

The flowing water can toss a floating body against rocks and tree trunks with enormous force. You should try to get rid of anything hindering you—like a backpack—and turn over on to your back. The safest things to try to grab are large rocks in a back eddy or tree trunks on the bank (see sketch).

If you are floating through rocks, point your feet downstream to avoid head injuries.

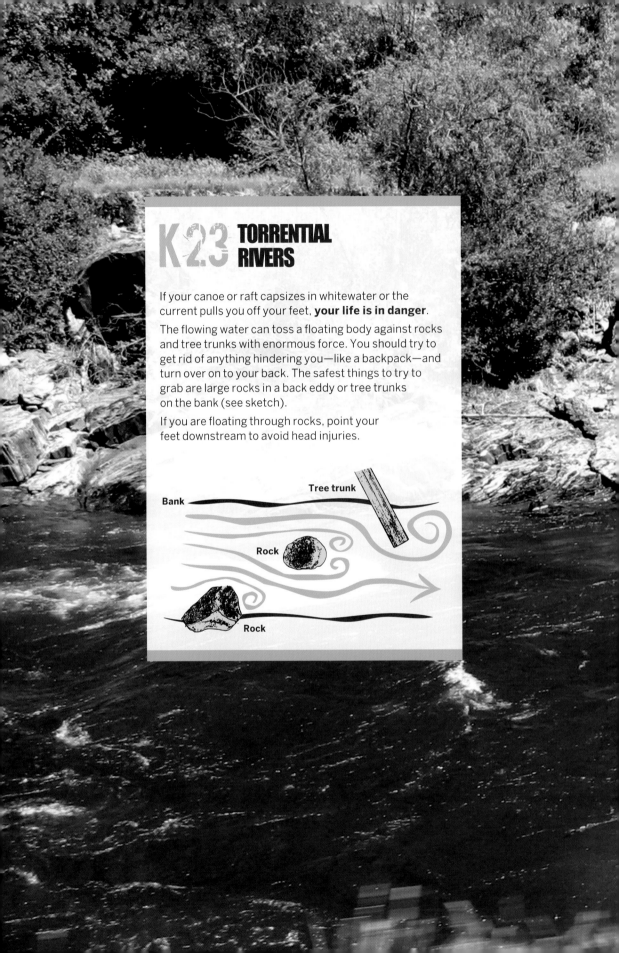

Bank

Tree trunk

Rock

Rock

M13 HEART-LUNG RESUSCITATION

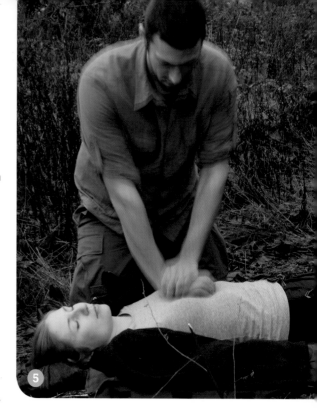

If someone has fallen in the water or is otherwise injured, cardiopulmonary resuscitation (CPR) can save their life. **The aim is to start the heart beating again.** Because all oxygen transmission through the vascular system to the organs is stopped by the loss of vital functions, cardiopulmonary resuscitation is usually combined with artificial respiration.

STEP 1 Remove the victim's clothing and lay them on their back on a flat and stable surface.

STEP 2 Kneel down next to the victim and stretch out their head. This clears the airways, which may be blocked by the tongue.

STEP 3 Breathe twice into the nose or mouth. This blows air into the lungs with light pressure.

STEP 4 Check artificial respiration by looking at the rib cage as it sinks again.

STEP 5 Keep performing chest compressions rapidly about thirty times (approximately twice per second). The pressure point is approximately the middle of the breastbone.

STEP 6 After every cycle, check whether breathing and heartbeat have started again.

STEP 7 If you are too tired or weak to perform artificial respiration and cardiac massage then only apply heart compression. Moving the rib cage will often aerate the lungs sufficiently.

3a *Breathe through the mouth by opening the jaw and pressing the wings of the nose together.*

3b *When breathing through the nose, the lips must be pressed together and thus closed.*

4 *Check breathing by listening (escaping air) and looking (rib cage sinking).*

R19 MAKE YOUR OWN SMALL HOOK HARPOON

If you have some fishing equipment but do not have any bait, or the fish are not biting, use a few materials to make a **small harpoon**, which can also be used to catch small pilot fish and other animals swimming beside your life raft.

What you need is an **elasticized band** (waistband or condom), a **hook** with some line, and a *spear* (tent rod, floating debris). Bend the hook forward, ideally into three prongs, and fasten it to the tip of the spear.

You should also fasten safety line to the hook, so that after the throw you can pull the spear out of the water.

If you get the harpoon tip directly in front of the animal you want, use the elastic band to accelerate the spear. Take note that you should be very careful when you use this technique from a boat or raft so that you do not damage the air chambers.

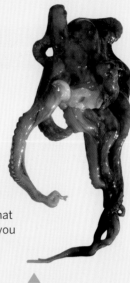

▲ Harpooned octopus.

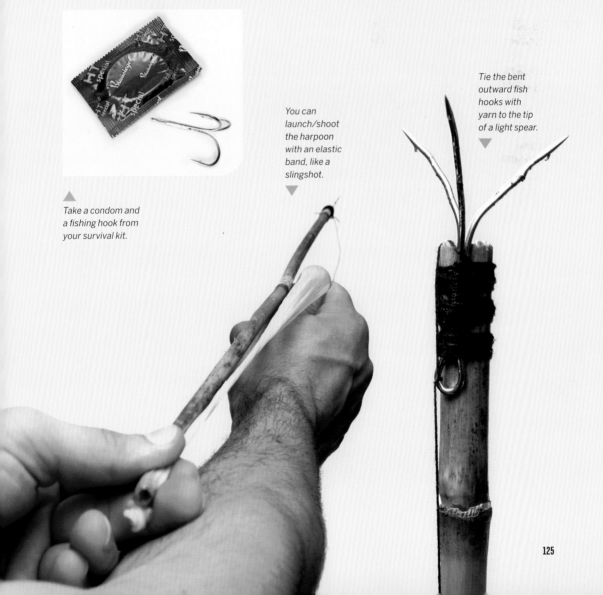

▲ Take a condom and a fishing hook from your survival kit.

You can launch/shoot the harpoon with an elastic band, like a slingshot.
▽

Tie the bent outward fish hooks with yarn to the tip of a light spear.
▽

W 11 TISSUE FLUIDS FROM ANIMALS

Virtually all vertebrates except sharks have a blood composition very similar to humans. **In an absolute emergency, you can drink "pressed water" from these animals.** Birds, land mammals, and freshwater and marine fish can all be used for this.

You cannot use the following marine animals as a "drinking water source": besides sharks, virtually all invertebrates, such as molluscs, snails, mussels, and jellyfish.

If you have to rely on animal body fluids for water replacement for a long time, you can very easily separate the proteins dissolved in the liquid (nutrient uptake needs water) by heating and filtering. High temperatures denature the proteins and they are no longer water soluble.

The remaining liquid from heated "animal juices" contains only small amounts of hard-to-remove dissolved salts and relatively small amounts of sugar and oil. Therefore, you can consider such liquid to be full-fledged drinking water.

K 2.4 IMPROVISE A LIFE JACKET

After capsizing, you might have to swim long distances. The greatest danger here lies in → **hypothermia**; over a longer time only a wet suit can reduce this. People also often drown due to exhaustion. Using the right method, you can keep yourself above water for quite a long time and thus get closer to shore. Turn yourself over on your back, because that gives you a chance to rest, and you get less water in your face. Breathe calmly. You sink slightly with each exhalation, but you can work against this by kicking regularly. If you see that you cannot reach shore by your own strength and have to keep swimming in one place for a long time, do the following: Pull off your long pants and tie the trouser legs around your neck. Now lift up the waistband and fill it with air and then push it under the water. When wet, the fabric is nearly airtight. This lasts for about five minutes. After that catch more air in the pants again.

M14 WATCH OUT, JELLYFISH!

Washed up on the beach—motionless and dead—poisonous jellyfish appear less dangerous than they really are. Jellyfish have poisonous tentacles with hundreds upon thousands of toxic cells that they use for defense and active hunting.

This lurking danger is especially great when you are swimming, or if your boat capsizes. These animals float invisibly under the water's surface. Any contact with bare skin causes painful "burns." **While lion's mane jellyfish give you an uncomfortable sting, other types can be deadly.** Sea wasps and the Portuguese man-of-war can cause life-threatening poisoning due to their microscopic harpoons that break through the skin and inject venom like a syringe. When touched, the tentacles sometimes tear off and stick to your skin. The stinging cells already released hooks firmly into your skin with barbs—they can no longer be removed.

Wash off any tentacles which remain stuck with urine or vinegar to deactivate the harpoons which have not yet ejected their poison. Under no circumstances should you try to remove them by hand or by rubbing. Without medical care, it is often impossible to treat the cause of the poisoning. After removing the tentacles you can treat the pain by cooling or applying a cream. The burning from the poison usually lasts a few hours.

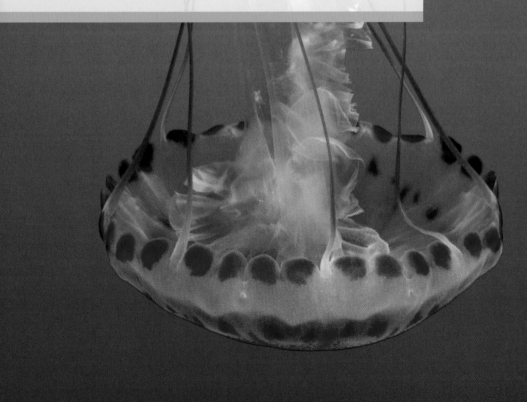

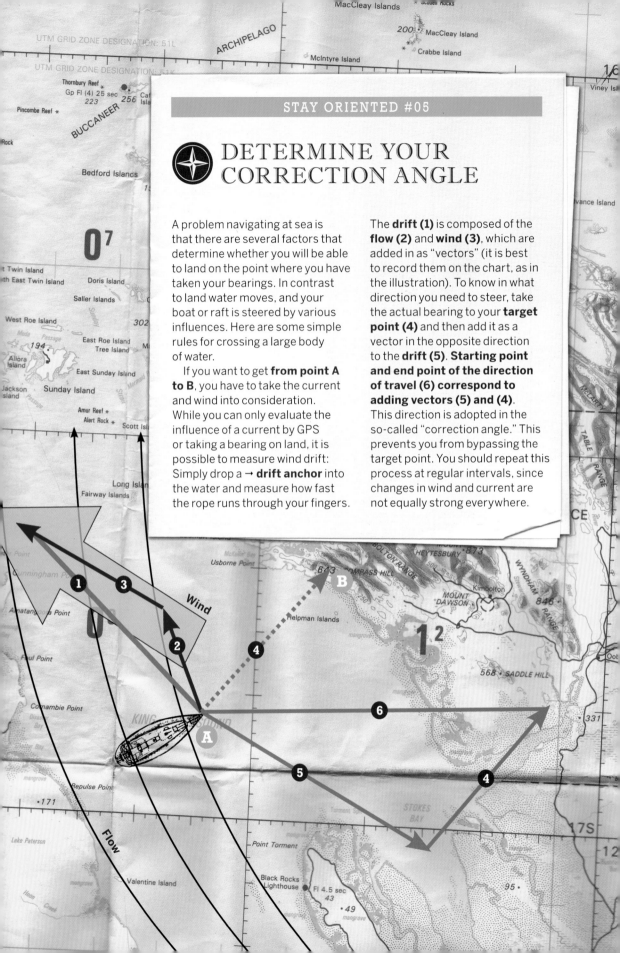

DETERMINE YOUR CORRECTION ANGLE

A problem navigating at sea is that there are several factors that determine whether you will be able to land on the point where you have taken your bearings. In contrast to land water moves, and your boat or raft is steered by various influences. Here are some simple rules for crossing a large body of water.

If you want to get **from point A to B**, you have to take the current and wind into consideration. While you can only evaluate the influence of a current by GPS or taking a bearing on land, it is possible to measure wind drift: Simply drop a → **drift anchor** into the water and measure how fast the rope runs through your fingers.

The **drift (1)** is composed of the **flow (2)** and **wind (3)**, which are added in as "vectors" (it is best to record them on the chart, as in the illustration). To know in what direction you need to steer, take the actual bearing to your **target point (4)** and then add it as a vector in the opposite direction to the **drift (5)**. **Starting point and end point of the direction of travel (6) correspond to adding vectors (5) and (4)**. This direction is adopted in the so-called "correction angle." This prevents you from bypassing the target point. You should repeat this process at regular intervals, since changes in wind and current are not equally strong everywhere.

A fly for fishing
at sea.

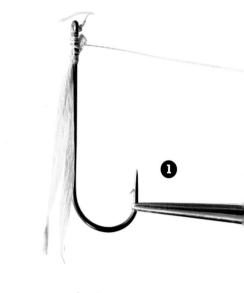

1

R20 HOW TO TIE FISHING FLIES

In the clear streams and lakes in the highlands live a wide variety of tasty fish, such as trout or grayling. Due to the clear water and the small number of fish living there, these fish are often adapted to snatching flies from the surface —they spurn worms and other natural baits. In this case you can tie a simple fly. You can use fibers from your clothes, feathers, and reflective foil (a corner of a rescue blanket).

Marine fish are especially tempted to bite by larger flies. To induce them, you can either land the fly on the surface or add some weight and draw it through the water as a so-called streamer.

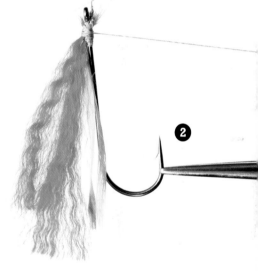

2

A fly to catch fish in clear rivers:

❶ *Fasten some yarn to a hook. Tie on the body of the fly (here made of natural fibers) by winding the yarn repeatedly around the hook.*

❷ *Fibers from your tent canvas serve as "wings." After they are tied tight, pluck at them so they stick up and sideways.*

❸ *Use some reflecting foil as "scales" to make the fly an irresistible bait for small fish of prey.*

3

R 2.1 FLOATING NOURISHMENT

Duckweed is one of the most common and important edible fresh water plants.

The tiny plants, less than half a third of an inch wide, consist of only a few leaves and roots. They float like carpets on the water of nutrient-rich ponds and lakes, and it is almost impossible to confuse them with anything else. They never display flowers—they reproduce by budding.

The plants gather a lot of starch. In autumn, they sink to the bottom, and rise to the surface again in the spring.

Duckweeds have some small "poison arrows" in their cells; if you consume too much this can penetrate the mucous membranes and cause severe abdominal pain. If you cook or scald the plants these harpoons are depressurized and pose no problem. Generally, you should cook all freshwater plants, because they can transmit parasites.

Two out of every three herrings (and many salmon) you have eaten were infested with anisakis. Had you eaten these raw and fresh, you could now be infected with this parasite.

▼

M15 BE CAREFUL WITH RAW FISH

Even if you have already eaten sushi in an Asian restaurant, in the wilderness—when possible—you should refrain from eating raw fish. **Saltwater and freshwater fish can transmit dangerous parasites.** Saltwater fish especially often carry nasty pathogens: Anisakis, worms that bore through the stomach and cause unbearable pain. In Europe, fish that are to be prepared raw have to be either frozen for two days or brined. Meantime, even in Japan fish is now treated this way.

▶

This little worm can make your life hell (image approximately life size).

K25 TURN A LIFE RAFT OVER

In an emergency at sea, life rafts can inflate upside down, and rubber dinghies can be capsized by a wave. Usually there are grips on the bottom side of such rescue units. Nevertheless, you should turn over the life raft as soon as possible. It takes some strength to turn over such a stable platform. If people are holding tight to various sides of the boat, they must (after being secured with a rope) let go of their grip. Lay a rope crosswise over the life raft— with boats lay it over the short side. Now one or more people should climb on to the platform, hold tight by the rope, and then tip themselves backward over the edge. If the rescue unit "comes along," pull up on the rope a little to keep the center of balance above the water. As the raft flips over you should jump away, so you do not get caught in lines under the water and so the bottom does not strike your head.

Self-inflating life rafts are standard equipment on larger yachts, cruise ships, and ferries. The rafts, packed in white barrels, are released by water pressure when the larger boat sinks, or by pulling on a ripcord.

▼

R22 IMPROVISED FISHING TACKLE

A fishing line every reader knows from the illegal fishing of their youth: A bent-over **needle as a hook (1)**, a **pebble as the sinker (2)**, and a **cork as a float (3)**. Since the hook does not have a barb, it is important to always keep the line taut when a fish bites. As soon as the cord goes slack the hook falls out of the fish's mouth.

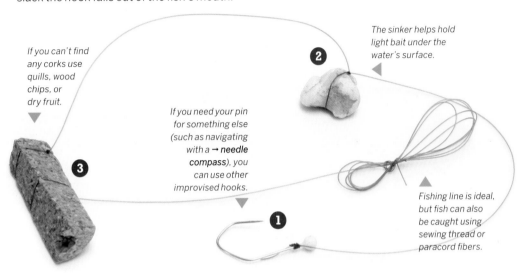

If you can't find any corks use quills, wood chips, or dry fruit.

If you need your pin for something else (such as navigating with a → needle compass), you can use other improvised hooks.

The sinker helps hold light bait under the water's surface.

Fishing line is ideal, but fish can also be caught using sewing thread or paracord fibers.

M16 REMOVING A FISH HOOK

It often happens while fishing that, due to careless handling, a hook gets caught in your finger or another part of your body. Since fish hooks usually have barbs it is hard to pull them out again. With eyeless hooks, remove the fishing line; with eyelet hooks or triple hooks, they have to be torn off with pliers **(1)** or broken through by bending them back and forth. You should disinfect the hook as completely as possible—at least clean off the bait and fish remains—and now you can push it out from the tip through the wound **(2)**.
   Wounds from a dirty hook must be examined regularly. If an abscess develops it must be → **lanced**.

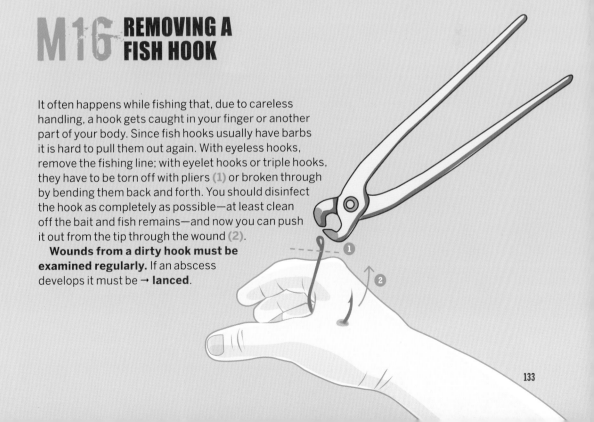

SLIP KNOT

If you want to tie a loop in your fishing line or clothesline a bowline will not work, because such cord is too slippery. So we use a slip knot for fishing.

STEP 1 Double back the end of the line; at least four inches (ten centimeters) of line must be doubled over. Hold the ends of the loop together.

STEP 2 Twist the loop slightly and form it into a ring. As with a double overhand knot, pull the loop end toward the bight.

STEP 3 You must draw the knot through the bight twice. Otherwise the loop will slip under pressure.

NOTE: Belay ropes, ropes, and cables should always be knotted into a loop with a figure eight or bowline knot.

1

2 2x

3

Cattails are easy to recognize. The fibers are super fire lighters. The rhizomes are packed with starch.

The lower parts of the stalk taste good and are tender when the plants are young.

R2.3 CATTAILS: STARCH BOMBS

Cattails have long and tapered leaves with parallel nerves (1). The leaves are folded tube-like into each other at the base. You will find a transparent mucus on the lower part of the leaves you have pulled out of the ground. The top third of the leaves, which are up to five feet long, is generally folded over. The surest way to recognize a cattail is by their flowers: At the top of the circular and hollow stalk sits a large brown ear made of parachutes pressed together. If the top breaks open a cotton-like mass emerges (2).

Inside this ear is a small, woolly, hairy stem which houses the pollen as the male flower part. You can also consume this until early summer. Cattails collect large amounts of starch underground and at the base of the leaves (3). You can eat the cooked leaf base as a starch-rich food. You can take out the starch stored around the fibers of the rhizomes and make it into flat cakes. The young leaves have a pleasant taste and are used like palm hearts (4). The flight hairs of the cattail are also ideal for lighting a fire.

R24 MUSSEL BBQ

You can often collect large quantities of mussels in fresh and salt water. Depending on the type and where you collect them, they can be delicious or taste awful.

Contrary to popular opinion, some mussels can move around actively and it can be a mistake to store mussels overnight in open water. They could be gone in the morning.

To find mussels, it is often enough to check the bottom side of a flat stone. It is also worth looking for them in the sandy bottom at the lake shore and in the silt between the fine roots on a bank.

In rivers, mussels like to hide behind large rocks in eddies where fine sand accumulates. If the water is very murky and the body of water is disturbed, you should not collect any mussels—they can be toxic.

Mussels are especially delicious when they are roasted in the embers.

Set them in the coals with the open side up. The heat makes them jump open quickly, and they can be eaten after another ten minutes on the fire. You can also simply cook them in water.

R25 WATCH OUT FOR POISONOUS FISH

If you are fishing, you have to be aware that there are poisonous fish all over the world. There are two dangerous types of scaly creatures: Fish with venomous spines, like the weever fish and scorpion fish, as well as fish which store poison in their body, such as puffer fish and salema porgy.

To avoid danger observe the following rules: All unknown fish could have poisonous spines. Never grasp a fish from behind with bare hands—at least wear gloves or use a towel to hold it. These poisons are no longer dangerous after they have been heated. However, most stored toxins are heat stable. Here, the rule is to always remove the organs as cleanly as possible from any unknown fish and never consume any fish that does not look like a "typical fish," which you do not recognize as an eel or catfish. That means any roundish, bristly, or trunk-shaped fish. In addition, the meat of large sharks is spoiled by ammonia and therefore cannot be consumed.

A boat made of sheeting and brush can be steered almost like a real canoe. ▶

You need at least one and a half times as many ounces of filling material as your weight in pounds. ▼

K26 AN IMPROVISED BOAT

If you want to keep traveling on a river or cross a lake, you can build a fairly sturdy and stable boat in less than an hour.

STEP 1 All you need is some plastic sheeting (fly sheet, tarp, poncho), which you spread out flat on the ground. Then spread plant material on it, such as nettles, scrub, or brushwood (but no thorns or spines).

STEP 2 Form the pile into a big donut shape, which you should press together lengthwise to make the final boat more steerable. Fold the plastic sheet back over this brush and there is your boat.

TIP: If you work some sturdy branches into the brush pile it gives the boat torsional rigidity, so you can steer it like a kayak.

K27 A TARPAULIN SAIL

You can make a sail from a tarpaulin and two branches or paddles. Fasten the upper end of the sail to the stern of the boat. Make the sail taut with a lateral boom and tie another corner to its end.

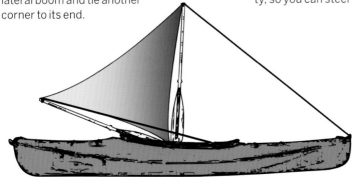

K28 CROSSING A RIVER

If you are in a swampy area or at a body of water, you probably do not want to have to take off your clothes and jump in the water each time you have to get across, especially since there are many dangerous creatures in the waters of the earth. To cross a ditch or river up to about thirty-three feet (ten meters) wide you can construct a rope bridge.

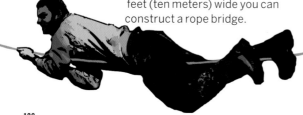

STEP 1 First, tie a static rope to the middle of a sturdy branch. Now wind the rope loosely around it, take the rope end with the branch, spin it around, and throw this anchor to the other side. The important thing is to throw the coiled bundle over the river—naturally keeping a good grip on the other end or tying it fast. It is best to try to land it in a fork in a tree, some roots, or the like.

STEP 2 If you have struck something, slowly pull on the line to wedge in the branch. When it is caught and stuck fast, lie down with your whole weight on the line to test if it holds.

Fasten a stick to the rope which can be thrown across the gap to make an anchor for the rope bridge.

To cross an obstacle on a rope bridge, lie down on the rope—it sounds at least as painful as it is.

STEP 3 Now look for an anchoring point on your side. About three feet (one meter) away tie a → **figure eight knot** in the slightly tightened rope. You can attach a carabiner or ring there as a redirector. Hang the rope on these after it has been fastened around the attachment point. Now trail it back and hang it on once again. This gives you a kind of pulley system which makes it easier to maintain tension. Fasten the end of the rope with a few coils and a → **half hitch**, but do not pull it quite through. This forms a loop (slip). When you arrive on the other side this lets you loosen your rope again so you do not have to leave it behind.

STEP 4 To get across, lie down on the rope so that it runs from your left shoulder over the navel and across the instep of your right foot (or vice versa). This lets you lie very stably on the rope and pull yourself forward. You definitely feel the forward movement in the crotch. It is best to tie on a scarf or something similar to relieve the pressure on the appropriate place. As you are sliding across, do not forget to take the rope end with you so you can release the rope from the other side.

This technique is also used when you have to wade through a wide, fast-flowing river, and there it is not high enough to let you crawl across. In this case hold tight to the rope, looking upriver, and cross the river moving sideways.

Large areas of rainforest still cover equatorial lands. While there are virtually no living creatures in the desert, the jungle is filled with life up to the treetops. Among them are a few animal and plant species that are dangerous to humans and can even cause death. Yet even today millions of people live in the jungle.

SURVIVAL IN THE JUNGLE

Green Hell

The sweat runs down between my shoulder blades into my pants and my poncho is glued to my body— it has been raining for hours. My feet are swollen, my shoes are wet, and my face and arms are pricked all over. For hours I have been working my way forward with a machete and am still in the same spot.

I feel as if I have fallen into an anthill, and yet I love this dark and dangerous place which is so forbidding and yet teems with life.

The tropical rainforests of this earth, together with the deep sea, belong to the last biospheres that mankind does not yet dominate completely. What counts here is the advantage of adapting better. Wild animals, undiscovered plants, and countless diseases await jungle hikers.

This environment, with its oppressive monumentality, keeps making it clear to me that, in the struggle for our survival, we humans will never prevail against nature.

E19 TROPICAL EQUIPMENT

If you want to hike in the tropical rainforest for an extended time, you can save a lot of time and nerves using some compact jungle equipment. This environment represents a special challenge. **The sultry heat, stinging insects, wet soil, rain, and poisonous animals can be dangerous.**

With a little practice, you can improvise some of this tropical equipment, such as making a rain cover from woven palm fronds or a makeshift → **hammock**. A water filter is not necessary if you can find or process clean water.

Your compact tropical equipment weighs less than six-and-a-half pounds and can be carried in a tiny waterproof backpack or a belt pouch.

Especially important and irreplaceable are anti-malarial drugs, which you must have for every jungle trip in malaria areas. **A single mosquito bite can transmit malaria**, and you will be stung constantly in the jungle, despite mosquito nets and repellents.

▷ *Lightweight tarp:*
You will always need this. If the heavens open up during a rest break or while you are sleeping in a hammock, it keeps you out of the rain.

Hammock:
Made of thin nylon or mesh material, it weighs only a few ounces.
▽

Insect protection:
Incense coils, mosquito repellents containing Deet, and malaria tablets are must-haves in the tropics!
▶

Light poncho:
Or raincoat, which also reaches over your backpack.
▶

Machete: *Buy it locally. The overpriced sheet metal bush knives you buy online are often unusable. You need: long and thin (crocodile) for scrub and lianas, and thick and bulky (parang, golok) for bamboo and undergrowth.*
▶

Airy, but sturdy and tear-resistant clothing: *Protects against mosquitoes, overheating, and scratches from the undergrowth when you are under way.*
▼

Mosquito net: *Separable from the hammock and can close tightly. You can use it not only in the forest, but also when you spend the night in a hotel bed.*
▼

Water filter: *So you can turn water from a tropical river into drinking water.*
▼

R2.6 SPIDERS AS EMERGENCY RATIONS

There are many spiders in the tropics. There are two groups of them worldwide which are easy to catch for food; they offer plenty of edible protein and are not very dangerous. You can find the large orb weavers between trees and shrubs. They are usually quite sedate and appear more dangerous than they are. The other group is the tarantulas, which move about in the undergrowth and under stones. You should not try to catch either with your bare hands, but strike them against the ground or chase them into an open area and there strike them against the ground with a stick or a piece of cloth. Cut off the front part with the globular eyes and fangs with a knife. The thick rear part with the silk glands can be eaten raw or grilled.

▲
Orb weavers are common worldwide and virtually harmless.

◀
ATTENTION! *Tarantulas have irritant hairs on their backs which they can release into the air when threatened. If you have to eat a tarantula, burn the hairs off the abdomen.*

E2.0 MYOG (MAKE YOUR OWN GEAR) ULTRA-LIGHT UTENSILS

In Asia, people traditionally eat with chopsticks. They are the ideal tool for picking up food when you have not washed your hands before eating. Chopsticks are the perfect eating utensil for backpacking, because they are lightweight and packable. You can also use the wooden sticks as a weapon (*kubotan*) to defend yourself in case an animal attacks. To make them, use some hard wood which has grown as straight as possible, about eight inches long and a quarter inch thick. Both sticks should be tapered evenly toward the tip.

✦ ORIENTATION USING A NEEDLE COMPASS

For production reasons, most small metallic objects, such as pins, paper clips, and safety pins, are magnetically polarized by induction hardening or a sorting system. Here I will show you how you can make a simple compass using these materials:

STEP 1 You need a container with water or oil. On the surface of the liquid place a piece of paper, a leaf, or some fabric.

STEP 2 Carefully place the metal piece evenly at the center of the float.

STEP 3 – IMPORTANT! Turn the float gently so that the needle has moved from its original position. Only if the needle again aligns itself in the same position can you be sure that the material is magnetic. The needle points in the direction of North/South or South/North. You also have to determine the precise alignment by the position of the sun or a similar method.

ATTENTION, MYTH: Metal cannot be electrically or magnetically charged by rubbing it on a cloth or some such thing, but a needle can be magnetized by a magnet (such as loudspeakers). Again, you must verify the polarity by the position of the sun.

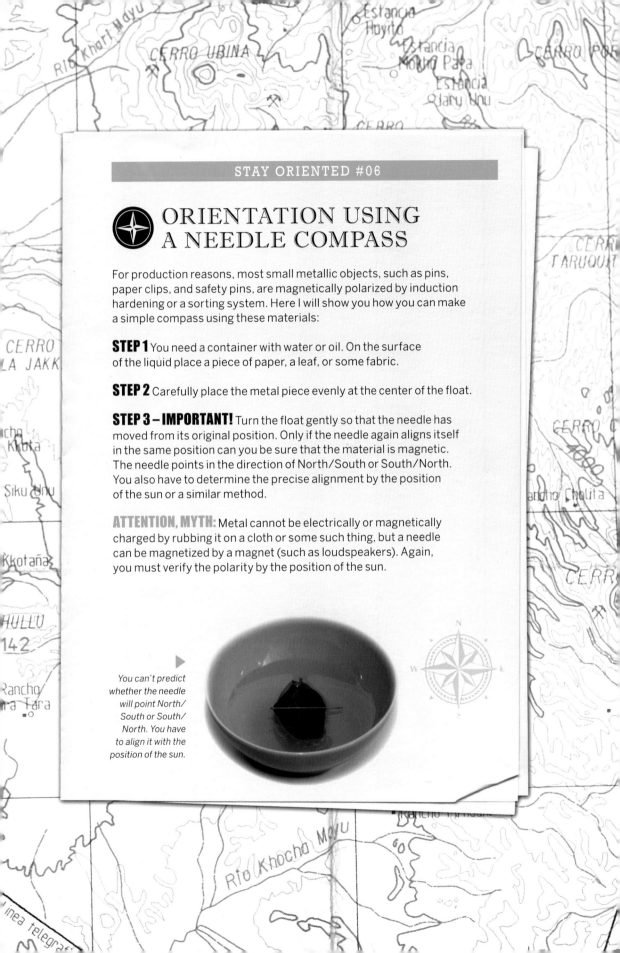

▶ You can't predict whether the needle will point North/South or South/North. You have to align it with the position of the sun.

F7 SAW A FIRE WITH BAMBOO

In all places where it rains regularly it is very difficult to ignite a flame without a lighter or matches. Wood that falls to the ground is soaked through and rotting. In the jungle, you often start a fire using bamboo.

Bamboo is a grass that can grow several feet high. If the stalks die they do not fall over; parts can remain standing upright for years, which is why their wood is mostly dry (except for the bent or cracked stalks).

Sawing a fire using bamboo is one of the most difficult methods. What you need, in addition to a large tube of bamboo or giant reed, is a slashing knife—you will not get very far with a simple carving knife with bamboo.

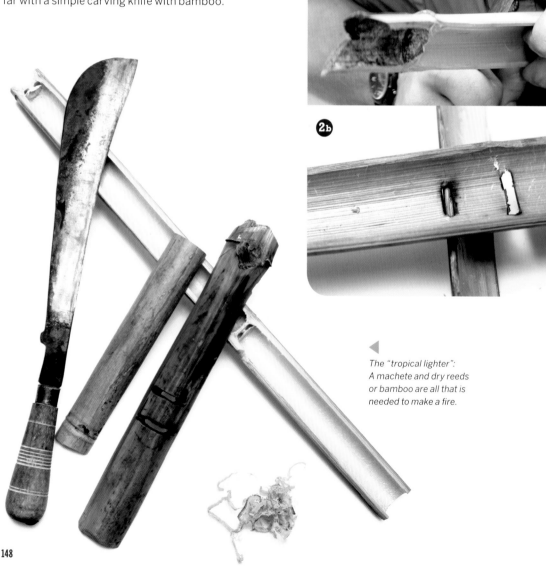

The "tropical lighter": A machete and dry reeds or bamboo are all that is needed to make a fire.

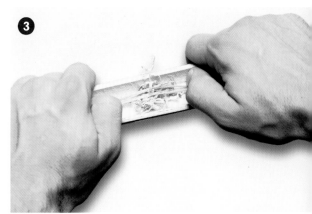

Rubbing a fire using bamboo from the tropical planting in your garden is the most athletic way to light a barbecue.

PREPARATION: You need a → **tinder nest** and an approximately three-foot-long piece of dry, hollow stem.

Split the stem. One of the two halves is the rubbing splint; divide the other in the middle. This makes the "fire board" and rubbing wood. The second half is rounded at the ends—otherwise, if it slips from your hands, the bamboo could stick in to your stomach.

STEP 1 Use the machete to scrape shavings from the bamboo. Hold the blade vertically and draw it in a scraping movement along the outside of a hollow stem. Also cut off a sliver from a small piece of bamboo to use later for holding the shavings.

STEP 2 a) Make a small horizontal groove in the rubbing wood. **b)** Later, this will be rubbed freely along the rubbing edge before the fire actually starts.

STEP 3 Put the shavings on the rubbing wood and hold them there with the sliver. Bend the sliver slightly so that the shavings are not flattened, but stay fluffy.

STEP 4 Kneel down and lay the rubbing edge on the un-worked fire board. Press with your chest to push everything down and stabilize it all against the ground.

STEP 5 Now use both hands to hold the rubbing wood with the groove on the rubbing edge. Push and pull the rubbing wood using vigorous body force rapidly along this edge. After a short time you will get dense fumes.

STEP 6 After a few minutes, carefully take away the rubbing wood and blow into the shavings—when they glow you can put them in the → **tinder nest** and ignite the fire.

THE TRIPOD
LASHING

In the jungle, it is often necessary to build a stable tripod for a shelter, or for holding up your backpack, because everything lying on the ground is quickly requisitioned by insects.

STEP 1 Use a → **clove hitch** to tie a rope to the top of a rod. Place a second rod next to it. At first you have to fasten the middle rod top down.

STEP 2 Weave the rope around all three bars a few times.

STEP 3 Rotate the middle rod so it is parallel to the other two. This puts a lot of tension on the knot.

STEP 4 Lash the end of the rope around the coils.

You can open up the tripod in any position (see above). This will again increase the tension.

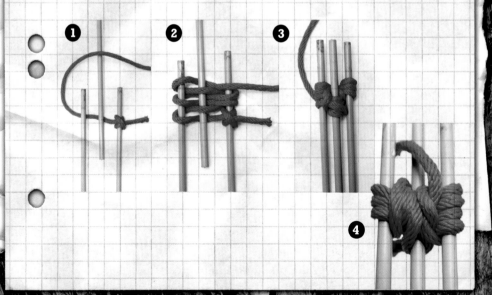

M17 TREAT DIARRHEA AND POISONING WITH CHARCOAL

Anyone who has eaten something unusual or tainted in the tropics soon suffers from "Montezuma's Revenge." The body uses vomiting and "flow through" to purge bacteria or toxins. Keep in mind that this can lead to severe loss of water and minerals, so it is important to consume salts and fluids. In addition, if you have food poisoning, you usually should not take any anti-diarrhea medication, since this could make you retain the bacteria and toxins in the intestine, which can cause severe damage.

It makes sense to administer charcoal, or—if available —medicinal coal. You need about three hundredths of an ounce (one gram) per two pounds (kilogram) of body weight for each treatment. Grind the coal to dust, stir it into water, and drink it.

◀ *Well-tempered charcoal: An effective drug.*

R27 A FORTIFIED SNACK

In warm regions there are many different species of grasshoppers. They are all edible, unless they secrete a malodorous secretion or are of a single color (yellow, red). Types like those shown in the picture at right can bite you badly or injure you with their rear legs when they jump. The latter are sometimes protected with very long spines and spikes that easily penetrate the skin. Prepare tropical locusts just like all other → **insects**.

▶ *I caught this creature in the Vietnamese jungle. It was so strong that, when I did not watch out for a moment, it was able to get its jumping legs loose and left me with a several millimeter deep, badly bleeding, and later infected slash wound.*

W12. FOG CATCHERS FOR DRINKING WATER

In the tropics humidity is extremely high. Since the temperature drops quickly at night you can collect drinking water even if is not going to rain for a few days.

Fog catchers should be as large as possible, sail-like structures into which water vapor can precipitate during the night. You can use tarpaulins, emergency blankets, cloth, shade nets, and metal foils which you suspend vertically between trees, on poles, etc. Water from the air prefers to precipitate on solid materials, such as on the fabric of fog catchers.

When the morning sun warms the air it also increases the air's holding capacity. Condensed water turns back to the gaseous state. To prevent this you must take down the fabric and wring it out before sunrise.

S7 WEAVE ROOF TILES OF PALM FRONDS

The rainforest is well named. Almost every day the sky opens up its floodgates and rain streams down for a few hours. So you will not get wet through in a few minutes —even in the jungle you can get hypothermia—you have to build a watertight roof over your head. If you have set up a → **hammock** and →**rain tarp** to outlast the downpour you have taken the necessary precautions.

If you do not have this equipment, you have to make a waterproof rain cover from the leaves of large perennials, or if those are not available, palm fronds, as the indigenous people do. Palm fronds have deep indents and are unsuitable as a roof cover. They must be woven into a solid thatch.

With practice this can be done so easily and quickly by hand that jungle inhabitants weave and build a new rain cover every night if they are on a journey.

In this part we will discuss weaving the "tiles" for the roof.

You can quickly weave solid baskets with palm fronds which can be used as a net for catching fish or crabs.
▼

STEP 1 Harvest the largest possible and preferably undamaged palm fronds. These are split lengthwise to give you two identical frond halves, each with half a midrib and the little palm leaves.

STEP 2 Then you start by bending over every second little leaf and turning it seventy to ninety degrees on the still untouched leaves. The little leaves of some palms fold themselves in when you do this, so take care to spread them flat before you fold them over.

STEP 3 From one side, start to interweave the little leaves. Take care not to let any mistakes creep into your weaving; always one over, then one under the next little leaf.

STEP 4 The little leaves remaining on the edge are bent over again and woven back into the web, creating a dense, basket-like surface. In nature, the individual little leaves are closer together than in the picture, where they are drawn apart to make the process easier to understand.

The upper third of the finished palm tiles are so dense that water dripping on them flows off without penetrating. If several are laid on top of each other you get a → **palm roof** that is absolutely waterproof.

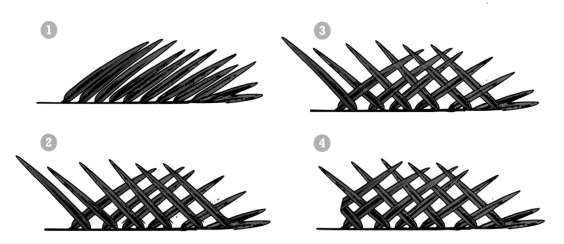

R28 PALMS AS FOOD

Palms grow in all warm regions. They can be distinguished from cycads because "real" palms (Arecaceae) never develop pine cone-like structures. You can eat the fruit of virtually every type of palm. Some of them produce a slightly euphoric effect due to arecoline when they are chewed with slaked lime (betel).

You will not find any strongly poisonous plants in the family of the date, coconut, and oil palms.

K29 CHASE AWAY MONKEYS

In the tropics travelers are often harassed by monkeys, who try to get at their travel provisions. Mostly monkeys make threatening gestures; it is rare for one to actually grab something. **Many species of monkeys can transmit diseases, such as rabies.** It is therefore important never to feed them. If they are still annoying, get yourself a branch about six feet long and strike the ground with it hard, right in front of the monkey. This usually scatters the animals.

It is important that you repulse the attackers courageously. If monkeys see that you are afraid or hesitate they will not run away.

F8 RECYCLING FUEL

If the wood in the rainforest is green and dripping wet the dung of large mammals is often the driest fuel. The dung of the rhinoceros, or as shown here the elephant, contains large amounts of undigested fiber. This dung does not burn properly, but smolders and provides a uniform heat for cooking or grilling.

The fumes, by the way, give your meat a very . . . interesting aroma.

R29 WIDESPREAD AND SHY

"Touch-me-nots" are herbaceous plants that grow all over the world, especially in tropical and subtropical regions. The impatiens most important for us have a flower that reminds you of an orchid. The complicated, usually yellowish or violet flowers are pollinated by large insects which want to get to the nectar gathered in small spurs at the end.

Their most important distinguishing feature is their glassy, hollow stems with thickened nodes, as well as the typical capsule fruits that explode at a light touch and disperse the starch-rich seeds. The lower leaves grow alternately low down; further up, they usually grow around the nodes (but only a few leaves) and are oval and pointed, with a serrated edge. Many impatiens are extraordinarily invasive species that spread quickly to new locations.

The very starchy seeds are particularly easy to collect by gently closing your hand around the capsule. The ripe fruits explode and leave the seeds behind in your palm. The Himalayan Balsam (impatiens glandulifera) is common in the Northern Hemisphere and can be found in big fields by bodies of water.

If you eat any part of all types of impatiens raw it will have a laxative effect, and in larger quantities will also cause vomiting. You can take small amounts (such as three to four lower stem segments per each six inches of height) for constipation.

▲

Impatiens flowers are a bit reminiscent of orchids. They can be purple, pink, blue, or yellow. The small "nectar spur" at the base of the flower is striking.

The fruits of impatiens are under pressure. When ripe, they burst at the lightest touch.
▶

The nearly round seeds, yellow if unripe and black when fully ripe, contain a lot of starch.
▼

E21 IMPROVISE A HAMMOCK

If you do not have a hammock but still do not want to sleep on damp ground, you can improvise one using your poncho and some paracord.

STEP 1 Use two → **clove hitches** and a → **square knot** to stretch a rope double between two trees.

STEP 2 Now cut two branches which you can insert taut between the ropes.

STEP 3 As in making an improvised stretcher, now wrap the poncho (if you lay down carefully and are not too heavy an emergency blanket will also work) around the ropes, so that it stretches tight when you lie down.

Depending on the width of the hammock and size of the poncho, you may still have enough material left over to wrap it over once again, forming a cover and protecting you from rain.

Clove hitch

E22 HOW TO CLIMB INTO A HAMMOCK

If you are not in the habit of lying in a hammock, you could easily climb into it the wrong way and end up making a back flip and landing in the mud. If you have a mosquito net, open it just about one-third of the way. If you are using one, zip open your sleeping bag along its entire length and spread it out so that it hangs down over the hammock side.

STEP 1 Now position yourself beside the hammock and put just the weight of half your backside on it. Everything will give a little.

STEP 2 Now carefully lift the leg next to your sleeping quarters and lay it straight on the mat. You still have one leg firmly on the ground and it will hold you if the hammock tilts. Now carefully lay down your upper body.

STEP 3 Take care that the mat has stopped swinging before you lift the leg still on the ground and finally lie down. With both hands on the edge, slide yourself so that you are lying slightly diagonally, comfortably and with your back straight.

Square knot

W13 EVALUATING RIVER WATER

You can drink clean river water anywhere in the world without purifying it, if the following factors apply:

1. The area is not inhabited by larger mammals, nor any ruminating livestock.

2. There is no settled area upriver from the place where you draw your water which might release untreated sewage into the river.

3. The water flows briskly, it does not smell foul, and the sediment near the bank is not colored black, nor is it slimy.

In any other situation, or if you are not sure, filter or boil water before drinking it.

M18 TREATING SNAKE BITES

In most cases snakes are shy and avoid confrontations with humans. You usually get bitten if you are trying to catch or kill a snake, or if you accidentally step on it, or touch one when thoughtlessly reaching into the undergrowth with your bare hands.

In the tropics, it is generally recommended you make your way "noisily" through the undergrowth. Snakes sense the vibrations and flee.

If you are bitten, you should clarify whether the bite is from a **(a) poisonous** or **(b) constrictor** snake. General handling instructions for all potentially serious poisonous animal stings or bites are:

1. KEEP CALM: presume the sting/bite was not dangerous, but nevertheless immediately treat it prophylactically. Agitation will enhance distribution of the poison in the body and can be the cause of various supposed poisoning symptoms, such as palpitations or dizziness. Only around thirty percent of all snake bites are by venomous snakes, and of these, almost half are "dry bites," i.e., no poison is discharged.

2. LIE DOWN HORIZONTALLY to avoid a fall due to losing consciousness, but do not raise the bitten body part above the torso. Remove all rings, scarves, bracelets, watches, etc., because they may cause deep constrictions due to swelling.

3. IMMOBILIZE WITH PRESSURE on the body part: Reduce lymph and blood flow by applying an elastic bandage or field dressing. Bind the area from the end of the extremity to the uppermost joint before the torso.

4. WATCH the injured person's vital signs. If unconscious, have them lie on their side.

5. IF NEEDED, ARTIFICIAL RESPIRATION: Some poisons may suspend breathing, although the heart is still working, and it may be necessary to give artificial respiration for several hours.

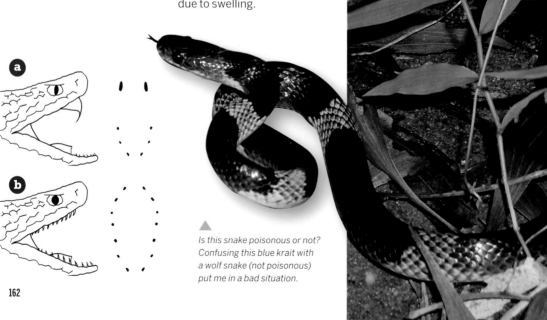

Is this snake poisonous or not? Confusing this blue krait with a wolf snake (not poisonous) put me in a bad situation.

S8 CONSTRUCT A PALM ROOF

You learned how to weave roof tiles from palm leaves in S 7 (page 154). Now you will use them to construct a rainproof roof.

There are different things to look out for when spending the night in a tropical rainforest.

At night, every conceivable insect, spider, and reptile will emerge from the dark corners of the ground in search of food. Any tent set up on the ground will often be occupied in no time by these jungle dwellers, so you have to set up a hammock or a raised sleeping area.

In addition, it can start raining at any time. So you will not have to spend the night being devoured by ants and soaked to the skin you can construct a frame using sturdy and straight trunks, bamboo, etc.

With the help of a → **tripod lashing** you can construct a pitched roof stable enough to support a hammock or camp bed. You can also put thinner rods on the broad sides of the frame. Lay a dense and overlapping roof of → **palm tiles** on top of these. If they slide down you can use → **clove hitches** to secure them.

You can also make a bed similar to the → **improvised hammock** by inserting sturdy rods halfway up.

You can build a rainproof makeshift shelter of palm trees and bamboo as quickly as a → debris hut, but you need a lot of practice.

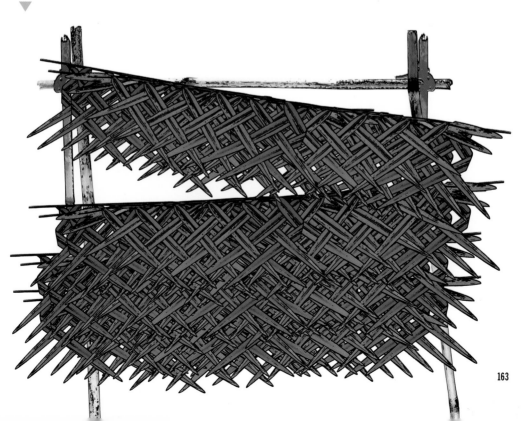

S9 SLINGING YOUR HAMMOCK

In the tropics people usually sleep in a hammock. You can put together your own tropical Sleep System. You will need a small hammock, a mosquito net against mosquitoes, and a tarp against the rain. First, look for suitable trees. They should not be too thick for you to sling the rope around, but not so thin that they bend over—they have to sustain a lot of force.

First, hang up the tarp. You should hang it up about three feet higher than the hammock. If possible, it should be stretched out on at least four points. If it sags, while it will protect you from the rain, the sleeping environment underneath will be unbearable.

Now you can sling the hammock so that you can spread out the mosquito net properly. You usually need about one and a half feet of "air" above and at least three feet beneath the hammock. The hammock should not be stretched too tightly: this will put a very heavy load on the rope, and second, if the rope is too taut, it is difficult to lie down in the hammock properly. It is best to hang a snap hook at the top of the hammock as a place to hang your backpack—close at hand, but off the ground.

▲
In the tropics, a combination of lightweight hammock and tarp make the ideal accommodation to protect you against insects and rain.

R30 USING A BLOWPIPE

People traditionally hunt with blowpipes in the jungle. Since the arrows deliver very little energy, they are poisoned with curare (poison from lianas). In an emergency situation, if you make a blowpipe from bamboo or a comparable tube, with the inner walls cleaned and burned out as well as you can, you should remember that you should only hunt small animals such as rats and mice with it, so that you can "nail" them to the ground and kill them right away. You can make arrows from bamboo splinters packed with wadding from a tampon or plant fibers.

After making the blowpipe and before using it to hunt, you should plan a few hours of intensive training before you shoot at animals— this also applies for an emergency. To shoot, load the arrows in the back end, set your target, and blow hard.

E23 HOW TO SLEEP IN A HAMMOCK

Anyone who wants to sleep in a hammock must be aware that you cannot lie down straight, as shown in the *Jungle Book*, but at a diagonal. The hammock must also be big enough and not strung too tightly.

Besides, due to the thin material and/or netting of your sleeping quarters, both the insulating material of your sleeping bag and your clothes will be compressed so tightly that they will hardly provide any insulation. Therefore, at cooler temperatures, you have to use a camping mat. In the humid jungle air you want a cooling effect.

In the cooler, higher-altitude regions of the tropical rainforest there is a trick: If you have a wide-cut sleeping bag, you can thread the hammock through the slightly opened foot zipper and then hang it up. When you climb into the hammock and pull the sleeping bag over you like a sausage casing it is much warmer than if you press the sleeping bag flat.

You should sleep at a diagonal in your hammock. This keeps your back straight and you lie comfortably.

R 31 SETTING SNARES

Snares set at small pathways through the bush almost always work successfully.

▼

In the tropics, every inch of clearing and small open space is overgrown. You can easily recognize pathways between the vines that small wild animals use to make their way through these obstacles. In an emergency you can set snares here and you can catch just about anything, from small rodents up to reptiles, which make their way along the jungle floor.

For a snare, use wire that is as strong as possible and tie it at the end of a stick with a double loop. This lets you twist the wire tightly. Pull the wire end through to form a noose. Set this on a pathway that is slightly smaller than the hole itself.

R 32 EATING TOADS OR FROGS?

Some toads with warty skin and large "ear glands" can generate deadly poisonous secretions, but there are also highly toxic frogs with no conspicuous warts.

▼

Since most amphibians cannot actively defend themselves, many frogs and toads have venom glands for protection. One of the best known tropical representatives is the poison dart frog. Therefore, the classification used in some survival books that "frogs are edible, toads are not" is incorrect. **All over the world there are many highly poisonous frogs, newts, and toads.** The best example here is the cane toad, which can grow up to ten inches long. It was introduced into Australia and is now dreaded due to its voracity and deadly poison. So you should only rely on Anurans which you know. Avoid warty animals and those that emit a milky or clear, bad-smelling, or conspicuously colored secretion in stressful situations.

If you have to rely on consuming unknown frogs, toads, or newts, you should at least remove the skin and thoroughly wash and rinse off the meat.

M19 SMALL BLOODSUCKERS

Many tropical travelers are afraid of leeches. In fact, they pose little risk. The land leeches you find in the tropics—or better said, the ones which will find you in the tropics—slip through every little gap in your clothes and then suck blood until they are many times their original size.

Except for the slight loss of blood, only the blood stains on your clothes are a bother. Although leeches, like all bloodsuckers, harbor a large number of pathogens and parasites, it is unlikely these will be transmitted by a bite.

To remove a leech, you can easily scrape it off with a knife or a machete. By the way, it is a fairy tale that leeches have a head that can tear off and continue to suck endlessly. You can usually just flick the leech off with your finger. Do not use the often recommended method of applying embers, salt, or acid.

Tropical leeches crawl through tiny holes and fatten themselves on your blood.

K30 TROPICAL KNOW-HOW: SIGNAL BINDING

Anyone who lets their tools fall to the ground in the tropics will have to spend a long time looking for them. To heighten contrast, all knives or machetes should be wrapped with reflecting orange cord (such as tent cords or paracord). This way you also always have a few feet of binding with you.

❶ *Lay a loop on the tool.* ❷ *Use the long end of the cord to wrap around the loop tip.* ❸ *Push the end through the loop.* ❹ *Pull hard on the lower end to tighten the coils.*

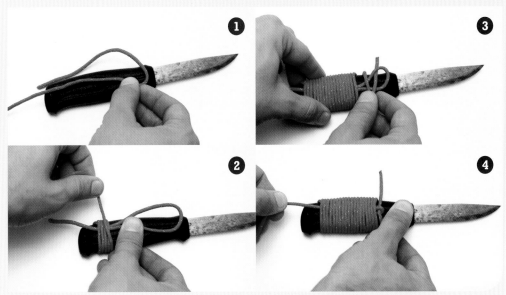

R33 FLYING SNACK

When he's hungry, the Devil eats flies (or beggars can't be choosers) . . . .

After dusk in the tropics it is very easy to catch flying insects. The creatures are magically attracted by light. If you light a fire or have a torch at hand you can hang a light-colored T-shirt or a rescue blanket between some trees and light it up. Within a very short time moths, flies, and other creatures[*] gather on the cloth, where they can be easily collected. For this reason head lamps are not always useful in the tropics—in a short time you have dozens of flies in your face.

* Due to the insects, for example, nocturnal giant huntsman spiders will also be attracted . . . .

E2.4 WORKING WITH A MACHETE

You have to be extremely careful as you cut your way through dense jungle with a machete. The machete is one of the most dangerous tools used outdoors. Accidents are relatively more frequent than when working with an ax. It is important that the machete is also suitable for your intended work. The "US machetes" or parangs available in Europe have little in common with real machetes. They are usually cheaply made and bend or even break, causing severe injuries. Especially if the machete is made of soft steel there is a risk that when you strike harder wood the blade will glance off and slip.

Thin and long machetes, like crocodile or bush machetes, are really only meant for cutting light vegetation like lianas and branches a few inches thick. Heavier and thicker machetes like goloks, parangs, or bolos are often a bit shorter and more top heavy, and can also be used on bamboo and other hard materials. Machetes are unsuitable for splitting wood.

When you strike, draw the machete diagonally in front of your body ❶. At the same time, hold your unused hand out of range in case the machete slips from your hand. The swing ends far behind the undergrowth. Strike the next blow diagonally in the opposite direction ❷.

**When you work with a machete,
you should observe the following rules:**

>> Make sure there is no one in
the danger zone.

>> Never work wearing gloves—you cannot
control the grip well and it can turn or slip
out of your hands.

>> If the machete has a retaining cord, never
put it around your wrist when working. If the
machete slips out of your hand it could
swing back at you.

>> Use machetes only for their
intended purpose.

>> Never strike at a flat angle, or the machete
can glance off.

>> Hold your unused hand behind your body,
like when fencing—this way a slip will bypass
your body without doing any damage.

>> As when using an ax, always use alternating
strokes (upward, downward) to strike at a
place or the machete will get stuck.

>> When cutting branches lengthwise, strike
the wood with the front quarter of the machete.
This has the most momentum and the blade
can cushion the blow—otherwise the
blade may break.

>> Do not use a machete after consuming
alcohol, when you are tired, or when it is
extremely cold.

>> Never strike in the direction of your
hand—even if it looks cool; if possible,
always place the work piece on the ground
or on a wooden block.

BLOOD KNOT

If you want to quickly construct a rain cover in the tropics and the guy ropes are too short, or when a fishing line breaks in the middle, you can bind smooth lines together with a blood knot, almost without a cross-over.

STEP 1 Hold the lines head to head against each another so that they overlap at least six inches.

Twist the ends around each other between ten and fifteen times. It is important to make sure the lines stay loose so that you can open a loop at the center of the coils.

STEP 2 Pass the ends of the two lines through the middle loop in such a way that the ends are threaded through from different sides.

STEP 3 Moisten the knot with saliva and slowly pull it tight (see image above). It is important to make sure the ends do not slip through the knot.

NOTE: After tightening the knot you can cut the ends short. This is especially useful if you want to mend broken fishing line.

K31 A BARRIER OF ASHES

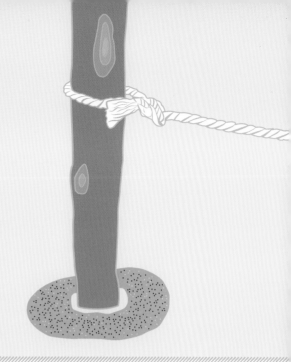

Moist wood ash is strongly basic (alkaline), and over a longer time as caustic as drain cleaner. A wall of wet ashes will keep snails, worms, leeches, ants, and spiders from raiding your camp.

You can mix wood ash with a little water and pour a ring of this around your camp, or at least around the trunks where you fasten your hammock.

M20 FOOT INJURIES

Injuries to the ankle and tibia are common in the tropics. Anyone who slips on a wet stone and falls over can break bones or tear ligaments. If this happens and you have to keep going, you need a supportive splint. You can make this out of single branches you bend around the foot and tie tight on the shin bone below the knee.

Before applying the splint, the support points must be padded. When the splint is fastened, you can walk without putting pressure on your ankle.

Bend thin and flexible branches to make splints and fasten them with padding under the knee. The many single twigs tied together can carry your body weight.

By the Outback, I mean not only the Australian bush, but also other places like the vastness of the African savannas and American prairies. This climate region is characterized by hot daytime temperatures and little water, but in comparison to deserts, they are home to relatively numerous plant and animal species.

SURVIVAL IN THE OUTBACK

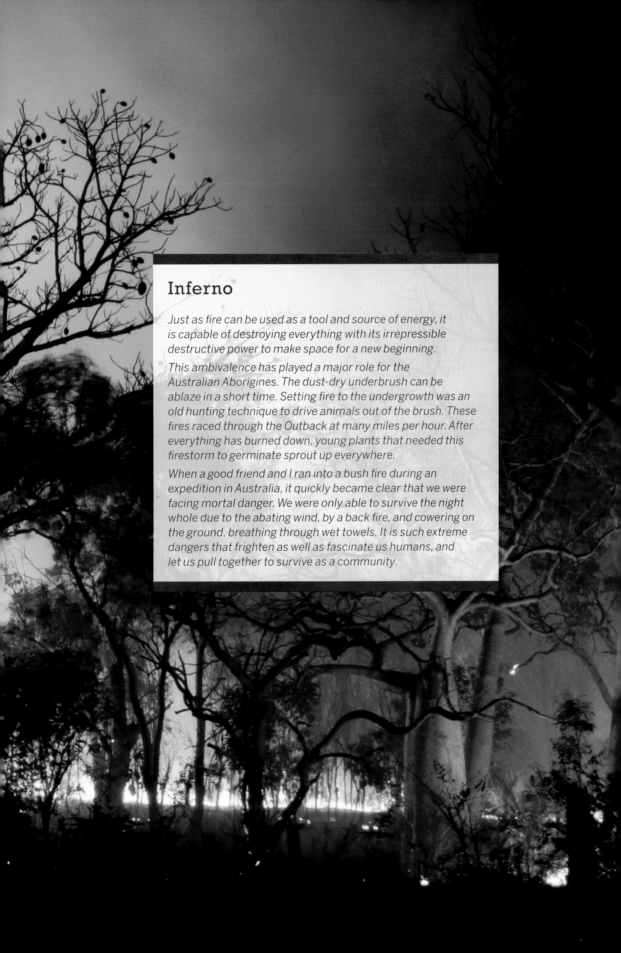

Inferno

Just as fire can be used as a tool and source of energy, it is capable of destroying everything with its irrepressible destructive power to make space for a new beginning.

This ambivalence has played a major role for the Australian Aborigines. The dust-dry underbrush can be ablaze in a short time. Setting fire to the undergrowth was an old hunting technique to drive animals out of the brush. These fires raced through the Outback at many miles per hour. After everything has burned down, young plants that needed this firestorm to germinate sprout up everywhere.

When a good friend and I ran into a bush fire during an expedition in Australia, it quickly became clear that we were facing mortal danger. We were only able to survive the night whole due to the abating wind, by a back fire, and cowering on the ground, breathing through wet towels. It is such extreme dangers that frighten as well as fascinate us humans, and let us pull together to survive as a community.

E2.5 EQUIPMENT FOR THE BUSHMAN

Steppes and savannas require relatively little specialized equipment, since you can improvise a lot using the wood and undergrowth already there. Nevertheless, the Outback places special demands on equipment for "Bushies."

Sharp thorns, prickly grass, and not least snakes and other creatures pose a challenge for your materiel.

▶ *Hat: A wide-brimmed hat protects your head from the heat and your eyes from the sun.*

Water kettle: Water should always be filtered or boiled in the Outback, because the livestock living there contaminate water holes.
▼

Water carrier: If you are not sure whether crocodiles or hippos will be inhabiting water holes you will need a pot with a handle and line.
◀

Boots: Sturdy leather boots, which can be quickly pulled off and emptied, are an advantage for hiking on fine sand mixed with gravel.
▼

▲ *Leggings: Spiky bush grass pierces any kind of pants. Leggings protect you from the spikes and snake bites.*

▶ *Bush knife: A lightweight and durable machete is the ideal tool to use on dry undergrowth.*

To hunt, throw a self-rotating kylie at the target (such as a flock of birds). Caution: A kylie does not return to you.

K32 CARVE A BOOMERANG

Not only in Australia, but in steppes all over the world, the boomerang—more specifically the kylie (a boomerang that flies straight)—is a common hunting weapon. Returning boomerangs were only used for duck hunting. Hunters whirled them over and over in circles above a pond; the ducks thought it was a bird of prey and ducked into the underbrush, where they could be easily caught.

If you want to make a kylie—a straight-flying boomerang—it is best to use a small tree that has grown on a slope, and so is curved and about two to three inches thick. In Central Europe and the US thick hazel switches are especially suitable. Look for a piece that roughly corresponds to a symmetrical boomerang shape and trim off the wood above and below. Now taper the curved spar on two sides down to about 0.4 inches thick using the → **power cut**. Round off the edges evenly in both directions. Carve the ends to a slight point.

If you want to make a returning boomerang you only round off the edge of the throwing stick on one side. This creates an airfoil that lets the boomerang fly in a curve.

R34 PLANTAINS: OIL RICH SEEDS

Herbaceous plants are rare on steppes and in semi-deserts. This makes it all the more important to be able to identify the ones that are edible. These include various types of plantain which are particularly robust and able to adapt.

Plantains can be clearly recognized by their approximate ten-to-twelve-inch-wide rosettes. The leaves are either oval or pointed. Typical are the ear-like flower heads that grow high above the rosettes, on which you can often find protruding stamens. You will not be able to recognize any distinct blossom on a plantain. After they wither, these plants provide many nutritious fruit capsules. Sometimes the whole plant is very hairy, such as the desert plantain or the psyllium.

Boiled plantain leaves taste quite bitter and can spoil all your greens by releasing tannins. They taste better raw. The young flowers have a nutty flavor and taste like mushrooms.

▲
The typical ribwort flower. The yellow tips are stamens.

▶
The broad-leafed plantain grows in the most unlikely places; a small crack in the asphalt is good enough.

▲
Edible plantains grow even in the steppes and desert.

The seeds of plantains contain oils and mucilage. You can use them to make a porridge and eat them like oatmeal.
▼

◀
The leaves contain tannins, which are useful against → insect bites.

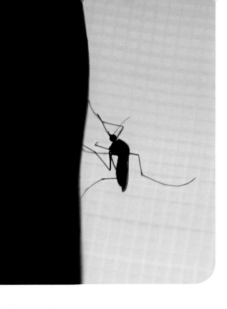

M21 TREATING ITCHING INSECT BITES

If you have been attacked by mosquitoes or stung by a hornet, your body responds with inflammation and increased blood flow to the bite. It begins to itch and swell. This is due to the enlarged blood vessels around the bite. You can treat these fairly simply by applying drops of sap from plants rich in tannins, including **plantains** (see left), **walnut**, **oak**, and many more.

IMPORTANT: **Do not apply plant sap to open wounds, only intact bites.**

K33 WATCH OUT, SALTWATER CROCODILES!

In Australia, Africa, and the Americas, as well as the coasts of Asia, there are large and aggressive crocodiles. Nile and saltwater crocodiles are "Natural Born Killers" that can heave about two-thirds of their body out of the water to grab prey. Once you are caught between the jaws of such an animal you have little chance. While the eyes of a crocodile are sensitive, many types can sink their eyes back into the sockets to eliminate any attack surface. Crocodiles bite into an arm or leg and turn it around its own axis with incredible force until they have taken off a bite—or they pull you right into the water to drown and wait until you have been tenderized by the tropical heat.

Never swim or bathe in crocodile-infested waters.

If you have to fetch water regularly from dangerous waters, you should always use different places to get it, or the animals will be waiting for you. Native inhabitants often throw little stones in the water before fetching water to check whether crocodiles are living in it. The animals have sensitive sensors on their snouts. If an animal is in the immediate area it will beat around with its tail and jaws.

You should not pass between the water and any animals lying on the bank. Crocodiles can sprint forward in a split second and push you into the water.

K34 LIFE ON THE STEPPES

Due to regular but low levels of rainfall, the steppes can maintain complex, albeit diminutive plant life. But you will not find large trees and a closed leaf canopy in this biotope.

Conversely, the animals that feed on these plants are very numerous, varied, and can also be, like lions and elephants, very large. Therefore, it is productive to collect the seeds of the abundant grasses and bushes as well as actively hunt.

K35 GROUND TO AIR SIGNALS

There is an endless list of visual signals that can be used to give signals at a distance. Therefore, it is better that you take good note of the main signs, rather than quickly look at fifty signs and forget them right away.

Interpreting signals for pilots is also sometimes difficult. Not every pilot knows the various military signals.

A generally valid and internationally understood sign for an emergency is SOS (Save Our Souls). Even a bush pilot in the South American jungle knows this one. You should also internalize some more signals that you can lay out using various materials in contrasting colors on the ground. Rescue blanket foil, tarpaulins, sleeping bags, and the like are suitable materials. If nothing else is available, signals can be also made from stones, sand ramparts, or plants. Especially when the sun is low, a raised surface will throw shadows that can be seen from a great height. Construct signals with a diameter of at least six feet.

▲
Depending on the size of the search area and surroundings, search flights can be done at altitudes from 1,600 to about 10,000 feet.

RESCUE SIGNALS

SOS
Danger, need help

I
Urgently need medical assistance

II
Need medical supplies

F
Need fire and water

LL
Everything's okay (if, for example, a helicopter flies over the camp during survival training)

I went this way (when you leave the area or the emergency shelter)

PERSONAL SIGNALS

Need medical help

Everything's OK
(wave with one hand)

Need rescue/transport
(both arms upward)

PILOT RESPONSES

(1) Rolling motion (flapping)
around the flight axis:
Understood.

(2) Full right turn and
flies over again:
Not understood.

In an emergency no more
communication is necessary.
It is enough if the pilot has
understood that you
are in trouble.

*Ground signals must be
constructed large enough
so that they are clearly
visible from a great height.*

FIGURE EIGHT KNOT

The figure eight knot is one of the most versatile bindings and can be used for climbing, sailing, and construction. With it you can fasten yourself to climbing ropes, knot a grip for climbing up a rope, etc.

STEP 1 Double the rope back over itself completely once to form a loop.

STEP 2 Thread the short end of the rope into the resulting bight so that the long end wraps around completely once. (This is the main difference from a simple overhand knot.)

STEP 3 If the knot is being used to make the rope thicker now draw that tight. To tie something on to a ring or a belt keep the knot loose.

STEP 4 Pass the short end through the desired attachment point. Now the complicated part starts: Pass the short end of the rope back through the still-loose knot the same way from which the knot originated.

STEP 5 Secure the short end of the rope on the long end with an additional half hitch when the knot is to be used for climbing, etc.

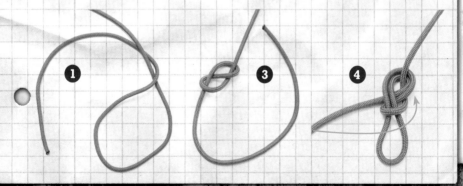

R35 USING FOUND DEAD ANIMALS AS EMERGENCY RATIONS

If you have to go looking for food when you are hiking, it can happen that you come upon a dead animal and have to assess whether it is still edible.

If possible, figure out the cause of death. **You should never handle any animals if there is no apparent cause of death.** This suggests a death caused by disease that could be potentially transmissible to humans.

If the cadaver is in a cold environment—below forty-one degrees Fahrenheit or even below freezing—it may still be usable for a few days to several weeks.

Rigor mortis is a fairly certain sign that death occurred a relatively short time ago. It is a clear indication of still-extant cell structure in the muscles. As decomposition progresses this stiffness disappears again. As a rule, animals with pronounced rigor mortis are still usable.

Another important test is examining the flesh. If it gives off a typical smell of death it is no longer edible. Bodily orifices provide especially good information about the condition. Test the mouth odor. The smell of death is evident here very early on.

If all other factors indicate the meat is edible, slice the meat with a knife and test the smell again. If the flesh is yellow-whitish, greenish, or slimy and frays as it is pulled apart, it is spoiled, but if it is red, dry, and firm it can still be eaten.

Thin pieces of flesh, such as ears or legs, dry quickly in high temperatures and can be eaten as natural jerky even months after an animal died.

W14 EXTRACTING WATER FROM PLANTS

If you find plants in the desert then they have at least enough water to live. You cannot get at the few drops that are absorbed through an extensive network of root hairs, but you can get the water directly from the plant. If you know the plant is edible, cut it into small pieces and extract the water by simply heating the plant material in a large pot. Like in a steam juicer, the water flows from the cells and can then be poured off. If you do not know whether the plant is edible or poisonous distill the liquid either in a pot or in a sand pit.

Edible plants lose their water through heating.

F9 BUSHFIRES: IMMINENT DANGER

The dry undergrowth of steppes burns rapidly in the summer. Bushfires can eat their way through hundreds of miles of country and burn everything in their path.

If you can see a bushfire on the horizon you need to start a counter fire fast. Ignite dry grassland on the downwind side. The fire burns the ground in a wedge shape, creating a safe zone where you can retreat after the soil cools.

R37 CUTTING UP A TURTLE

You can find turtles in any hot region of the world. They live in water or on land and are easy to catch.

To prepare a turtle after killing it, set it on its back and remove the lower shell (heavy stone or sturdy knife). Now cut out all the intestines and stomach from the animal. Then simply place the turtle on the coals like a cooking pot.

F10 RUBBING FIRE

In many hot and dry regions, it is often not easy to find the right material for drilling a fire with a spindle. In the tropics you use bamboo or reeds to → **rub for embers**; on the steppes and deserts often sticks are rubbed together to make a fire. The basis for this is the fact that a bushman always has a sturdy and hard piece of wood at hand, such as a digging stick or boomerang. In fact, most wood tools in the Outback are multipurpose tools. The boomerang is thus used not only for hunting or as a club in armed conflicts, but is also for digging and as a fire saw. The digging stick is used to dig out animals; if they flee, the stick is used as a hunting club.

For a fire saw, you need a hard piece of wood with a sharp edge and a softer piece that does not necessarily have to be wood—it could be dry palm fronds, dead cactus, etc.

Use →**wooden wedges** to partially split the softer wood. It should not break into two pieces, but just have a gap about a 0.4 in. wide. Stuff pieces of tinder which will ignite quickly, such as airborne seeds or animal manure, into the gap. Anchor everything stably on the floor. Then rub the hardwood edge with moderate force and at high speed along the edge for quite a long time. The resulting friction is far less than you get with a fire drill. After five to ten minutes (!) you can take a break and see if you can fan the dust heap so it starts to glow. If this does not work after several times in succession, try doing the last rubbing strokes with more force and at a lower speed.

If the material starts to glow put it carefully into the → **fire nest** and blow on it.

R38 PREPARING BIRDS

Especially in the steppes, birds are one of the few safe food sources. Nests can be found near the few water sources, and birds can be caught with a slingshot, boomerang, or with fishing line and hooks.

Immediately after killing a bird you should remove the crop, which is on the neck between the breast muscles. There are seeds and insects inside that can spoil the meat if they ferment.

Before they are gutted, which is done mainly the same way as → **gutting mammals**, birds should be plucked. The best way to do this is heat a pot of water, but do not let it boil, then turn the bird upside down and start to pluck it. Scalding makes plucking easier, and fleas and other parasites can't jump out at you. Pluck large feathers with the grain, small feathers and down against the grain. In between you can briefly scald the animal from time to time.

R39 CLUTCHES OF BIRD EGGS

It is usually easy to reach bird eggs that have been laid in a nest on the ground or in a hole. Sometimes eggs are very well camouflaged. If you come too close to the nest, the parents often make a racket a little way off to distract you. Waterfowl also unintentionally reveal their nests: they literally play the dying swan and flutter awkwardly around on the water—all just show. If the waterfowl has lured you from the nest it makes a vertical take-off. Do not let yourself be put off and look around the area where the drama began. Unlike eggs from the supermarket, those you find in nature will practically always have been incubated; at times there will be a more or less formed embryo in the chalky shell. While this may be visually daunting, nevertheless they are very tasty! Bird embryos have no hardened bones or feathers. In Asia they are often eaten as a delicacy.

W 15 WATER HOLES

The rare places where water is always available will be visited by a variety of large and small animals. The problem here is the dung of ruminant wild animals. These animals transmit protozoan parasites that can cause severe diarrhea, including cryptosporidium and giardia, which survive the normal levels of chlorine and ozone used to disinfect water. For this reason you should definitely filter or boil water from water holes, or you have to allow for the longer time the water disinfectant needs to work.

K37 WHEN YOUR VEHICLE GETS STUCK

It can often happen that your vehicle gets stuck in the sand. It is important that you immediately stop giving it gas when the tires start to spi, otherwise you will dig your car in.

If you do not have a sand ladder to put under the tires you can manage with a floor mat, camping mat, sticks from dried-out trees, and the like. If the transmission is already in the sand you have to remove the sand under the car with a shovel or cooking utensils and turn the tires in the direction of travel. If that still does not work, let a little air out of the tires—to 1.5 bar minimum. This increases the contact surface. You can also use a → **Swiss pulley** to apply tension to the vehicle.

If your car is totally stuck in the desert you should **always remain at the location, or at least stay within sight!**

1. *Reduce air pressure.*
2. *Dig the tires out.*
3. *Lay down something for traction.*

R40 GOOSEFOOT AND SALTBUSH

On reclaimed land goosefoot, saltbush and foxtails are the first plants that form a stable population. All three are among the very common edible "weeds" that also grow on steppes and in deserts. The flowers are small clusters of heads in the upper part of the plant, which is often branched. The seeds are sometimes sharp-edged, but are usually soft. Chenopodium (goosefoot) and saltbush usually have alternating foliage, which sometimes has silvery hair, and the form is either goosefoot-type **(3)**, lance-shaped, or slightly arrow-shaped.

Since it is often difficult to loosen the seeds from the flowers, simply cook the small flower heads and swallow them after chewing them well. You may confuse an unknown saltbush with the mercurialis, or dog's mercury plant. Take note that goosefoot and saltbush have leaves distributed irregularly around the stem, while the dog's mercury leaves grow across from each other.

K38 WOODWORKING WITH A STONE

Many trees in deserts and steppes grow only a few millimeters a year due to very rare rainfall, so the wood is extremely hard. Desert ironwood is a classic example. It is so hard that it is worked using iron filings and a hacksaw.

If you want to make a digging stick, boomerang, etc., from such hard wood, it makes sense to spare your knife —it could be damaged by the tough timber.

Instead, you should look around the area for some flat, rough stones. Sandstone, for example, is very suitable. Break the stone at various places.

With any luck you will get yourself a real knife edge that you can use to ram against or saw into the hard wood fibers. Since the breakage of the stone edge created several different angles you can also use these as a "set of files" of various shapes.

You can easily file notches in the wood with suitable angles, for example, to make a trap.

This technique not only lets you work on very hard wood, it is also extremely helpful **if you have lost your knife.**

M22 TREATING AN ABCESS

If you get stuck with a thorn or have a broken-off splinter an abscess can develop. This occurs relatively frequently outdoors. An abscess is an enclosed inflammation under the skin that keeps expanding and can break open internally. To prevent this, you have to puncture or cut open the abscess. It is best to use a sterile scalpel or a clean, disinfected knife. If you do not have any further treatment options, you should just cut into the skin at the inflamed site and then gently press on the wound to open it.

A mixture of water, blood, and pus will drain out of the opening. If you have water purification tablets, dissolve two in a glass of water and use the water to clean out the wound cavity.

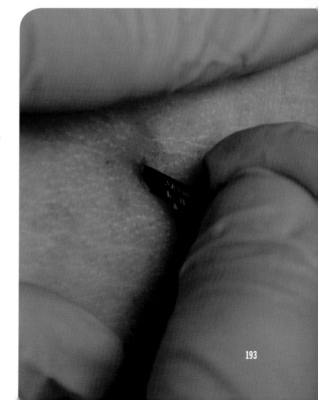

If you are looking for attributes of the gravel, sand, or salt deserts of the world, "dead" would be an obvious concept. And yet a number of animals and plants have adapted to the harsh life there. Humans can only survive in the desert for a few days without equipment and supplies. Here only preparation, strategy, and appropriate action can prolong life.

SURVIVAL IN THE
DESERT

Contrasts

*People do not travel to deserts to get there,
but to tackle the desert and themselves.*

*The hostile aura overlays every rock and every grain of
sand as a shimmering midday heat. It is precisely this
forbidding attitude of the desert toward us living beings
that is transformed into its opposite when we reach an
oasis, a small waterhole, or the first village.*

*The exuberant life, lush greenery, and twittering birds
and animals which quench their thirst here are all in stark
contrast to the gray boulders and the hard-baked sand,
where in the daytime only spiders, scorpions, and snakes
survive. All larger animals remain hidden under stone slabs
and in caves until the coolness of the night comes.*

*To appreciate and experience this, it is not enough to visit
the desert in an all terrain vehicle; you have to master the
desert with the strength of your muscles.*

E26 DESERT EQUIPMENT

Since there is very little wood and almost no water in the desert, our endeavors are restricted to moving forward as efficiently as possible, saving water, and avoiding getting too hot.

Beyond what you do to store water or take water along on a handcart (→ **sulky**), equipment is limited mainly to protecting yourself from the sun and heat.

In addition to the objects shown here, you need as backup, depending on the temperature at night, morning, or evening, and during the midday heat, a → **tarp**, a sufficiently warm → **sleeping bag**, plus a → **camping mat** and optionally a tent and sand tent pegs.

Sunglasses: Normal sunglasses are usually adequate for deserts (exception: deserts in the mountains → *glacier glasses*).

Cap: A cap with a neck shield and long brim protects against sunstroke.

Light clothes: Fabrics that are light and as light-colored as possible of cotton or synthetics reduce the risk of heat stroke.

Pulse or neck cooler: This fabric tube is filled with very strong water-binding crystals. If they absorb water or urine they cool for several days.

Transparent water bottle: Helps control water consumption.

Turban: An approximately six foot long sturdy cloth that serves as an under layer and can be wrapped around the head in sandstorms.

S10   SPENDING THE NIGHT IN THE DESERT

It can get very uncomfortable in the desert at night. Once the sun has set, it is usually much colder than during the day. Temperature differences of more than 86°F are not uncommon. Due to these temperature swings it often starts to storm very badly. A very small tent pitched with the short side facing the wind is ideal for the desert.

Sturdy tents, like those used in the mountains, are sufficiently storm resistant, but it is not always easy to stretch the tent ropes tightly enough. It is best to look for a place as sheltered as possible to pitch your tent. There is often much less wind behind rocks and stones, or if you are sheltered by

a dune. All equipment should be tied fast before nightfall. The wind does not have to be that strong for it to blow your equipment away; if it is hidden by morning by a thin layer of sand you will never find it again. At night you should also have a towel within reach. A storm can drive tiny sand particles through the smallest gap in a zipper. You can cover your face with the towel and sleep peacefully.

You can secure the tent ropes with sand pegs. Cut a long piece from bamboo, reed, or a plastic container and attach a loop in the middle—set it on its concave side and dig it in slantwise.
▶

R41   EATING ANTS

All over the world you can find ants under every stone, under bark, and in trees. The little critters build entire countries underground, where they rear eggs and larvae. If you can dig out a nest, or lure the ants out of their building, you will have found something to eat. The white larvae are especially delicious and provide energy. Collect the ants and larvae in a pot and simply put it half in the shade. The ants will move the larvae and eggs to the shaded part. This way they clean your lunch of sand and dirt. It is important that ants absolutely must be heated before you eat them. Not only can they transmit parasites, but **some have a wasp sting and can sting you in the mouth!**

THE BOWLINE

With the bowline knot, you form a loop that does not pull tight even under the weight of a load. It is the **car-towing knot** you can easily untie again.

STEP 1 Tie a noose through a ring, a loop, or around a tree, for example. Now wind the long end into a loop. Do this exactly so that the back part of the loop is the long end.

STEP 2 Now pass the short end from behind through this loop. There is a memory rhyme for this: "A snake comes out of the pond—crawls around the tree—and then dives back into the pond." So in this second step the "snake" has come out of the pond.

STEP 3 Now draw the end of the rope just a little through the loop, pass it from behind around the long end of the rope, and from above back into the loop (. . . crawls around the tree—and then dives back into the pond).

STEP 4 Now tighten the bowline evenly. The excess amount should be the length of at least ten times the rope diameter. Secure it with a → **half hitch**. Now you can fasten a load to the knot on the long end.

STEP 5 To loosen the tightly drawn knot pull the long end toward the bight. You can now slide the knot toward the rope's end and untie it.

❶   ❷   ❸

R42. NUTRITIOUS GRASS SEEDS

Grasses quickly shed their seeds when they ripen. You should be sure to harvest them when they are still unripe. All grasses, with a few exceptions, are edible. You should avoid types with very small seeds, because these may include some that are inedible.

▼

Grasses are one of the most widespread plants in the world.

You can recognize grasses by the stalk, which is the same thickness its entire length, and is either round with nodes (grasses), round without nodes (rushes), or triangular without nodes (sedges). We are interested in all species of small grasses, regardless of the category to which they belong. You certainly know some of the cultured forms as rice, rye, or oats. For wild-growing grasses what is interesting for us is the large amount of energy stored in the seeds. You can often harvest big fields of grasses on riverbanks or at the forest edge, and even on steppes and in deserts. Since the wild types tend to shed their seeds when ripe, if you are seeking food, you should also gather unripe seeds.

Some fungi which grow on the grains of some grass species pose a certain risk; these can contain strong poisons, called **ergot alkaloids**. When you are gathering seeds look for black fruiting bodies of small fungi—avoid any infested plants.

Since it is hard to remove the entire husk from these grains, pound them **on a hard surface with a wood or stone pestle**.

You can gently blow away the loosened husks. Mix the flour into a thick paste with some water and bake it into "crackers." You can eat the meal raw or cooked in soup.

Grass seeds vary widely in size. Wild grains such as emmer or einkorn still have the largest grains.

▶

K 39 WHAT TO DO IN THE DESERT

In the arid and inhospitable deserts on the Earth only those who have prepared well, have adjusted well, and act correctly survive. Most important to focus on:

PREPARATION: You must calculate your daily drinking water intake and carry that amount along for each day. For safety, you should set up marked water reservoirs along the route. At least one week before starting your desert trek you should get acclimated locally and train in the prevailing heat.

EQUIPMENT: You should transport large amounts of water on a → **sulky**. Take as little gear as possible. Light-colored clothes prevent the body from overheating in sunlight. Only inexperienced beginners wear black clothes in the desert.

ADAPTATION: Hike in the early morning and evening. Avoid the midday heat. Breathe calmly and steadily. If you move too fast you will sweat too much.

W16 DRINKING BEYOND YOUR THIRST— HYPERHYDRATION

If you drink more water in a hot climate than you need, or your mineral intake is too low, **"water intoxication" can be a threat**. Symptoms of this imbalance of your internal mineral and water levels can include headaches, dizziness, and vomiting, as well as such serious symptoms as impaired consciousness and convulsions due to a life-threatening edema in the brain.

It is important to pay conscious attention that you get an adequate salt intake. An ideal solution when you need a high water intake is to add extra salt to your food, eat salted meats, or suck on salt tablets.

W17 SAND PIT DISTILLATION

By using sandpit distillation you can harvest water even in the low humidity conditions in the desert if you have a plastic sheet or rescue blanket available.

Dig a pit as round and as wide as possible in the ground. In the middle set a pot with a hose—if you have it—for siphoning off drinking water. Cover everything tightly with sheeting.

Use the tarp, ideally a transparent type, to cover the pit and bury the edges so it encloses the air space in the pit tightly. Lay a stone

▶
You can use plastic sheeting to harvest water from sand and poisonous plants.

in the middle of the sheeting, directly over the pot. The sunlight and greenhouse effect will make it extremely hot inside the pit, and water from the sand or from parts of plants you toss into the pit

will condense on the sheeting, from where it drips into the pot. If you have salt or dirty water available pour this on the ground around the pit or, if amounts are small, sprinkle it into the pit before closing it.

A canopy suspended double over a sand pit protects you from the midday heat.

S11 STRANDED IN THE DESERT

During your trip through the desert, if you are left with no or only very small reserves of water and it is impossible to find enough liquid water you are in a water crisis, and you can only delay dying of thirst.

These situations often occur if you get stuck in the desert in an all terrain vehicle or it breaks down. Eventually your water runs out. The main rule is: **Stay with the vehicle.** Here you have equipment, partial shade, and material for a signal fire. In addition, your vehicle can be seen from an airplane—a person alone will get lost in the wilderness. In a water crisis, the highest principle is **to keep your water consumption as low as possible.** You have to greatly reduce the amount of water you need to cool the body. You must absolutely ration any drinking water you might harvest or still have.

Basically, you have to ensure your exposure to heat and movements is reduced to a minimum. During the day, rest in the cool shade and put off all absolutely necessary work to the cool of the night. If you have a tent or blanket available hang it up as a double-layered canopy, forming an insulating roof. In gravel and sand deserts, dig as deep a pit as possible *at night* and drape the protective roof over it, keeping it ventilated during the day. Body heat will be drawn up from this pit. During the day rest in the pit.

You must absolutely avoid overheating and sunstroke. Do not speak or eat, just "vegetate" in the shadow and hope you will be rescued. In this state a few drops of morning dew or some timely collected urine can prevent dying of thirst for a few days. **Here every drop really counts.**

M23 IMPROVISED SUN PROTECTION

If you have used up all your sunscreen you will always have to avoid the sun, unless you make your own. You can use all substances that either reflect or can cover the skin so that light cannot penetrate.

White ash from a campfire is one of the most reflecting materials. Mix this with → **melted fat** or water and apply the paste; it will reflect a good part of the light away from your now silvery, gleaming skin!

You can also use coal, sludge, or sap from plants, such as walnut, which have a tanning effect. Naturally, these will give you a different adventurous look than if you apply glistening ashes to your face.

K40 PREVENTING SUNSTROKE

Near the Equator, when the sun is high the rays fall almost perpendicular to the ground. So while the rays just "glance off" other body parts when you are standing upright or walking, full sunlight strikes your skull, neck, and shoulders. The resulting heat effect can cause sunstroke.

While the core body temperature is raised only imperceptibly, the brain overheats, causing it to swell. Sunstroke can be recognized—assuming the head has already been exposed to the sun—by oppressive pain in the skull, nausea, and vomiting. Treat this illness by getting into shade immediately. If this is impossible because you are in the desert or paddling across a lake, cover your head loosely with a damp cloth or hat. To prevent sunstroke in advance you should usually wear a hat or loose head scarf (turban, *shemagh*) in hot regions.

▲
ATTENTION! *In some countries, a shemagh is seen as a sign of political views. There it is best to use a white shawl, which is also a good heat reflector.*

HOW TO WRAP A SHEMAGH (TRIANGULAR SCARF) FOR SUN PROTECTION

STEP 1 Fold a shemagh in half to make a triangle.

STEP 2 Put the scarf on your head, leaving one side a bit longer than the other.

STEP 3 Now wrap the shorter end under your chin and fasten it.

STEP 4 Next pull the long end over the short end to the other side of your head.

STEP 5 When you have wound the long end around your neck tie both corners together.

A cloth wrapped this way not only protects you from sunlight, but also from sandstorms, hail, etc.

THE SQUARE KNOT

You can use the square knot to tie two equally thick ropes together and thus extend them. Please make sure when using this knot that both ropes have the same diameter and are equally flexible. If one of the ropes is too stiff or thicker than the second, the square knot will form a →**lark's head knot** and slip right off the rope.

STEP 1 Start the knot with a simple overhand knot (simple knot). Make sure the ends are long enough.

STEP 2 Now cross over the rope ends so that the second overhand knot is tied in exactly the reverse way, forming a double knot.

STEP 3 Make sure that both the long or the short ends are all on one side. Now tighten the knot slowly and evenly.

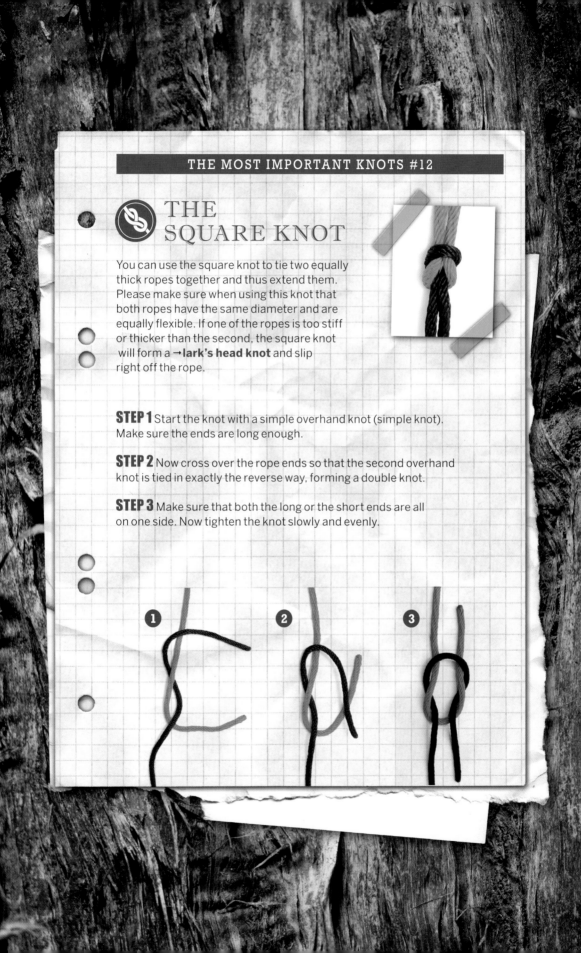

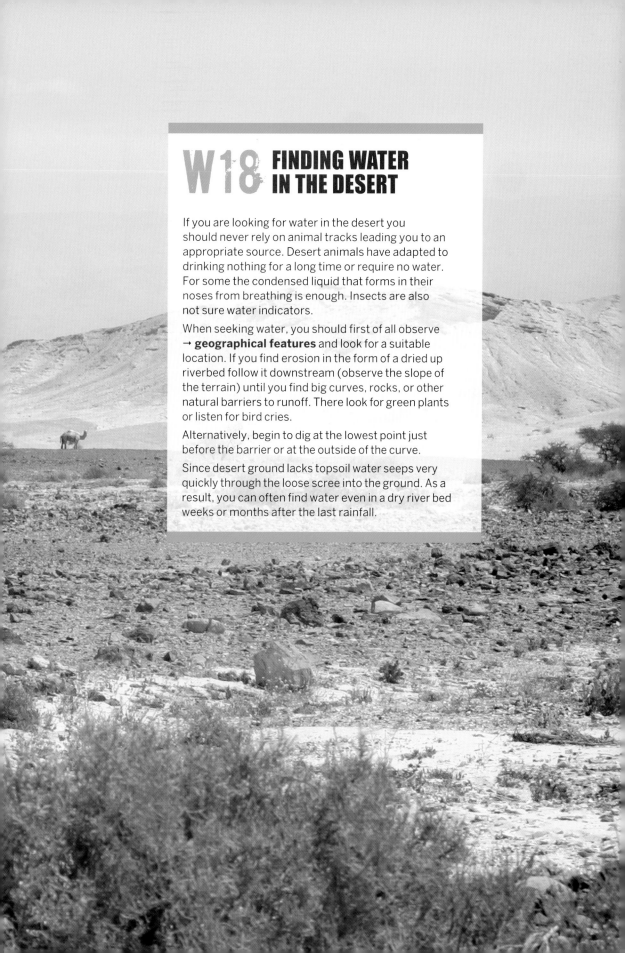

W18 FINDING WATER IN THE DESERT

If you are looking for water in the desert you should never rely on animal tracks leading you to an appropriate source. Desert animals have adapted to drinking nothing for a long time or require no water. For some the condensed liquid that forms in their noses from breathing is enough. Insects are also not sure water indicators.

When seeking water, you should first of all observe → **geographical features** and look for a suitable location. If you find erosion in the form of a dried up riverbed follow it downstream (observe the slope of the terrain) until you find big curves, rocks, or other natural barriers to runoff. There look for green plants or listen for bird cries.

Alternatively, begin to dig at the lowest point just before the barrier or at the outside of the curve.

Since desert ground lacks topsoil water seeps very quickly through the loose scree into the ground. As a result, you can often find water even in a dry river bed weeks or months after the last rainfall.

E27 CONSTRUCT A SULKY

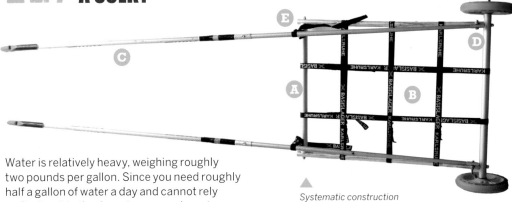

▲ *Systematic construction of a sulky viewed from above.*

Water is relatively heavy, weighing roughly two pounds per gallon. Since you need roughly half a gallon of water a day and cannot rely on finding it in the desert, you may have to take along more than three and a half gallons of water per week. You can hardly carry this sloshing mass in your backpack. A sulky, or pilgrim's wagon, which you can load with water bags and draw behind you, is ideal for the desert. You can buy a sulky in a specialty store, or with a little skill you can make one from a child bicycle trailer or scooter. Take note that two-axle trailers are always better than single-axle ones; in difficult terrain you should stress having a sturdy drawbar and large wheels. To build a sulky you need a stable frame (A) that you string with cloth or belts (B) so water bags can go on top. You can make suitable drawbars (C) from carbon ski poles. Reinforce them at the tip with a metal sleeve and bore a hole so you can bolt them to the sulky (D). You can make the second suspension point (E) from straps.

Always make sure everything is screwed together with self-locking nuts and that baggage can be lashed on so it will not be lost.

A sulky for a flat desert with no sand and rocks.

R36 EVENING PRIMROSES: QUEEN OF THE TWILIGHT

You can process the oil-rich seeds and nutritious roots into a paste.

The first thing you will notice about the evening primrose is likely to be the sometimes very large, cross-shaped, brightly colored flowers. The leaves of the evening primrose are usually oval and pointed, and are always distributed irregularly around the stems. It often forms a rosette of leaves at the base which springs out of the stem, which usually has no branches and is slightly woody. There are flowers or large fruit capsules in almost all of the axils of the leaves emerging from the stem. The capsules are upright, and when ripe contain large numbers of fawn-colored seeds.

Evening primrose usually blooms from the bottom up, so that a plant usually already has large quantities of almost ripe capsules while the upper flowers are yet to unfold. The sticky, cobweb-like pollen can be clearly seen hanging from the stamens. You can find various kinds of evening primroses all over the world at dump sites, on riverbanks, and in woodland clearings.

K36 DIGGING STICK— YOUR FIELD SPADE

To dig edible roots or larvae out of the rock-hard baked desert soil you need a sturdy digging stick. These are found in many different climate zones and can also be used in the forest to pry out and split wood.

You should give yourself some time to make a digging stick. It must be cut from very hard wood or ground with a stone if you do not have a knife at hand. A universal digging stick has two different tips: A blunt one for scraping and digging and a much stronger squared tip (like the tip of a → **wooden tent peg**).

A special feature for making a digging stick is that after shaping each sharp edge, you again shave or plane a strip from the edge to slightly round it all off. Otherwise, any sharp parts will get bent over and hinder your work when you are digging—mud and sand will get stuck there.

Finally, harden the tips a bit in the fire. Rotate the tips in moderate heat until they are reddish-brown.

▲

To make sure you do not get yourself into trouble in the desert, you should set up water stores or have a → **sulky** along.

W 19 STORING AND RATIONING RESERVES

My rules for using water on extreme trips in deserts and other water-deficient regions:

>> Even if you can replenish your water every day, always have at least a quarter gallon as an untouched reserve.

>> Start rationing as soon as you can see that your available amount of water is too low—**not just when the water starts to run out.**

>> As soon as it is clear that, despite reduced consumption, you cannot reach your goal with the water available, drink as little as possible.

>> When you break open the last half a gallon of your "iron reserve" start to reduce consumption significantly—now you should drink a maximum of half a cup of water daily.

S 12 PULLING THROUGH SANDSTORMS

In desert regions, especially in spring and summer, hot winds can raise sand or dust storms.

As menacing as the dark wall rolling toward you is, the storms are not dangerous if you take correct actions. Since you can see practically nothing you should not drive your vehicle during a sandstorm, but look for a place to park beside the road (there are always those who are incorrigible and try to race with sand storms). If you are walking, you should set things up for yourself for a few hours. It is hard to pitch a tent during strong and fast-gathering storms. What you can do is wrap your → **shemagh** over your eyes, sit down somewhere, and wait. You will not get buried.

E 28 ON THE ROAD WITH A SULKY

Anyone seeking the ultimate border crossing between life and death is well served by a fully self-sufficient desert trip.

You take your water—your life insurance for the entire journey—along with you. While it is impossible to carry enough water even for three days on your back in a hot and dry climate, a sulky can make it possible to travel on foot in areas that have never before been entered by a human being.

You can carry up to twenty-six and a half gallons of water on a sulky. Before you plunge into an adventure with a → **self-built sulky**, you should absolutely test its reliability on similar terrain and work out how long a stretch you can manage with it during a day.

If you are taking very little equipment along besides water you can cover a distance between twenty-four and thirty-seven miles, depending on the ground and how fit you are.

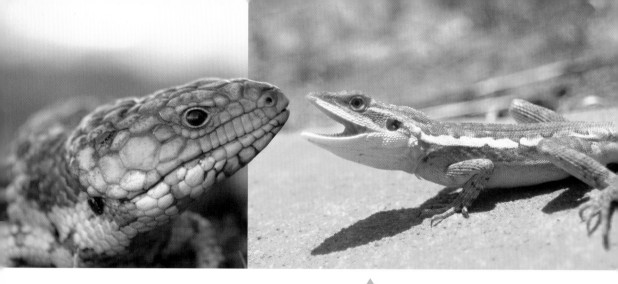

▲
They are not poisonous, but can bite pretty hard. Reptiles should generally be killed with traps or a club, and in no case caught with bare hands.

R43 EATING REPTILES

Reptiles are used as food all over the world. While →**snakes** can defend themselves with poisonous bites, four-legged species such as turtles, lizards, and iguanas are usually harmless. Of course, any type can bite you, but except for one Central American lizard they have no fangs. Because the saliva of large reptiles such as monitor lizards is heavily permeated with germs you should absolutely avoid being bitten.

The easiest way to trap such animals is in a →**Pajute death trap** using old fish as bait, or by striking them with a long branch.

After gutting you should prepare them right away, because their flesh spoils quickly in the heat.

W20 DRINKING URINE

Even if you may have already heard otherwise, urine is not a suitable liquid to drink if you are dying of thirst—but beforehand, it is.

If your blood has a sufficiently high water content, the kidneys excrete urine which contains plenty of water and has a low *mineral concentration*. This transparent urine has a low concentration and can be used as drinking water. However, if the body has too little water in the blood due to dehydration you excrete concentrated urine that is "denser" and a deep orange, almost reddish color with a small amount of water and a lot of salts.

If you drink this when in danger of dying of thirst the results can be deadly, just like drinking salt water. If you have no more water available from one day to the next, depending on the climate, you can still collect urine for about twenty-four hours as a drinking water replacement. Later on you can no longer drink urine without → **distilling** it.

SWISS PULLEY

If your car is stuck, you want to lift a heavy load, or have to hoist an injured person out of a crevice, a simple pulley with a blocking knot can help.

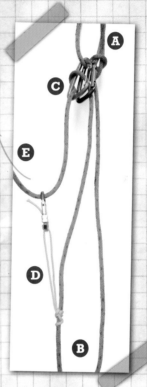

STEP 1 Tie the rope to a tree or hook and fasten two carabiners in the loop **(A)**.

STEP 2 Guide the rope around a redirect point on the load **(B)** and draw it back to the knot on the fixed point. Here the rope is looped into the hooks as a → **garda hitch (C)**, so that the rope can be pulled, but does not slip back when the strain is eased.

STEP 3 A few feet away use a → **prusik sling** to make another redirect point **(D)**, in which the free end of the rope is suspended.

If you draw on the rope **(E)** now you have to apply only a fraction of the force necessary for lifting or pulling the load.

If you stop to rest the garda hitch acts as a block and the load will not slip back. If the prusik reaches the garda hitch it is pushed back toward the load.

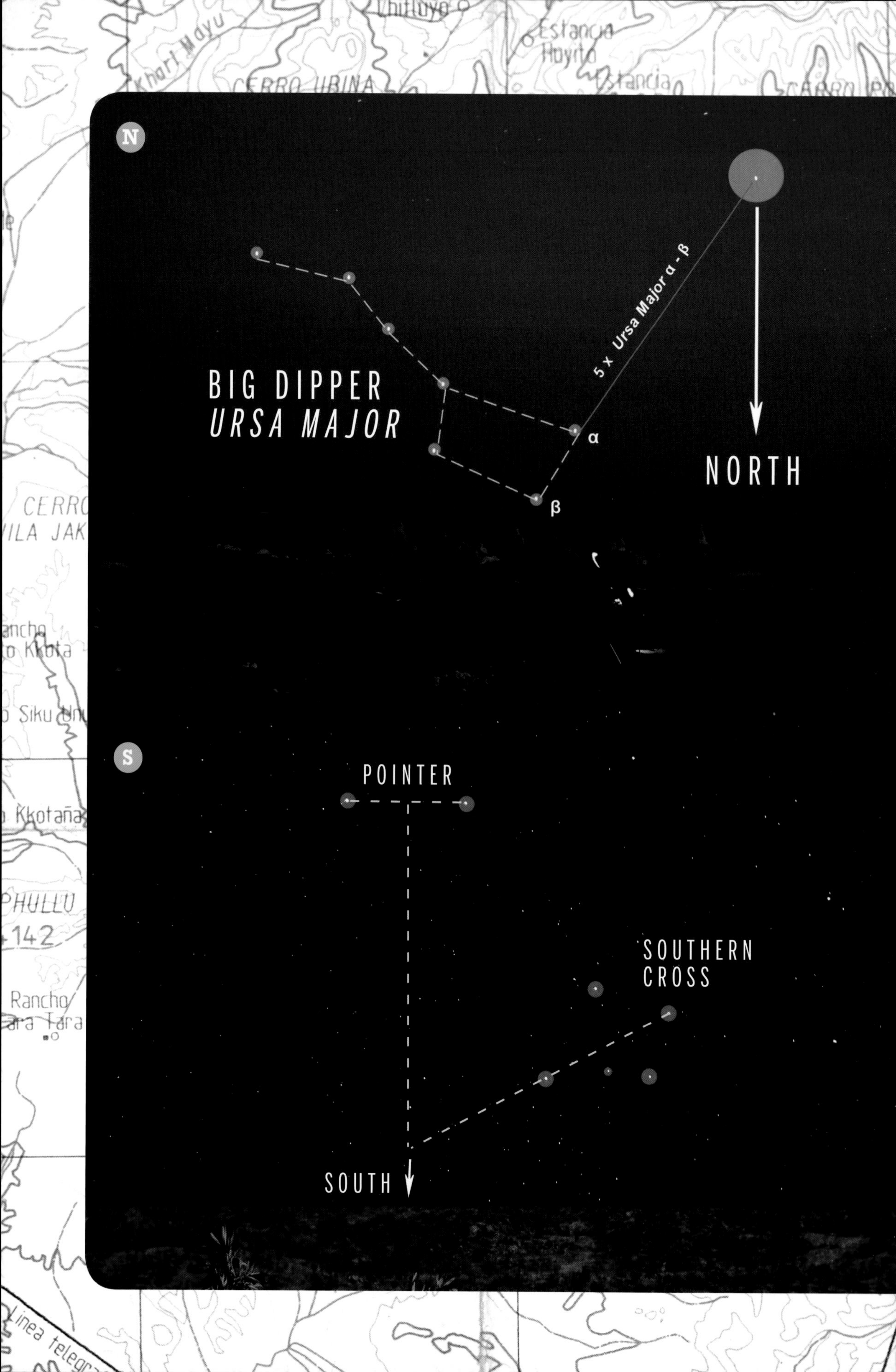
N
BIG DIPPER
URSA MAJOR
5 x Ursa Major α - β
α
β
NORTH
S
POINTER
SOUTHERN
CROSS
SOUTH

⊕ ORIENTATION UNDER THE STARRY SKY

In an emergency, to be able to define your direction of march in an unknown environment, you must at least determine the cardinal points. At night, this is easiest with the help of the stars. Depending on whether you are in the Northern or Southern Hemisphere, you will work with the help of the constellation **"Big Dipper" (Northern Hemisphere)** or the **"Southern Cross" (Southern Hemisphere)**.

Ⓝ NORTHERN HEMISPHERE

STEP 1 Search for the trapezoid of the Big Dipper (also: "Great Bear"). In temperate latitudes this constellation is visible the entire year.

STEP 2 Find the last two stars "α" and "ß" on the lower side of the dipper.

STEP 3 Imagine the line connecting "α," about five times the length, to the nearest bright star (Polaris, or the Pole Star).

STEP 4 Draw the shortest (perpendicular) line from Polaris to the horizon. This position marks the North.

Ⓢ SOUTHERN HEMISPHERE

STEP 1 Search for the "Southern Cross" and the two bright "pointer stars" shining in its neighborhood.

STEP 2 Extend the long part of the cross to the horizon.

STEP 3 In thought, connect the two pointer stars with a line and draw a vertical line in the middle.

STEP 4 The extension from the cross and the vertical to the "pointer" connection will intersect.

STEP 5 Draw the shortest connection (perpendicular) from the intersection of the two lines to the horizon. This position marks the South.

Who hasn't dreamed of living as a trapper in their own log cabin, cooking over the fire and living by trapping and selling furs? To get a sense of this way of life you do not have to move to Canada right away; your little garden shed or barbecue hut are already a good start. You can learn all the techniques and practice them there, then someday perhaps even spend an entire year in a lonely forest cabin.

SURVIVAL AS A TRAPPER

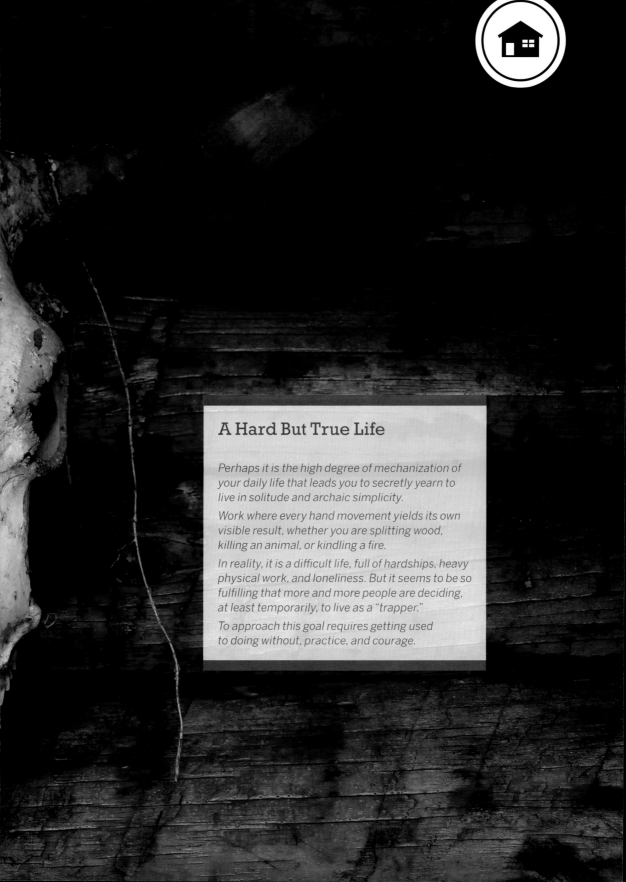

A Hard But True Life

Perhaps it is the high degree of mechanization of your daily life that leads you to secretly yearn to live in solitude and archaic simplicity.

Work where every hand movement yields its own visible result, whether you are splitting wood, killing an animal, or kindling a fire.

In reality, it is a difficult life, full of hardships, heavy physical work, and loneliness. But it seems to be so fulfilling that more and more people are deciding, at least temporarily, to live as a "trapper."

To approach this goal requires getting used to doing without, practice, and courage.

E29 THE TRAPPER'S EQUIPMENT

You will certainly not arrive at your trapper's hut on foot. Usually you transport your working materials by boat, plane, or all terrain vehicle.

A trapper's life is tough, so you can let yourself enjoy a little luxury and romance. You will be able to take a lot more along besides the equipment described here, but the following are essentials.

▲
Dutch oven: Use a cast iron pot to cook directly over the fire. Whether for beans with bacon or game, a Dutch oven helps you cook everything successfully.

▶
Candle lantern: A lantern with a spring-loaded candle stylishly lights up your hut at night.

▶
Kelly Kettle: A double wall kettle works particularly well for brewing your morning coffee quickly in camp; it works by the stack effect.

Fire piston: You can light your campfire or pipe in proper style with compressed air, without using gas or matches.

▽

Leather gloves: A trapper frequently works and cooks over an open fire. To keep everything under control, protect your hands with heavy leather gloves.

▽

Ax: For splitting wood and fallen trees a high quality wrought iron ax works best.

▶

F11 CHOPPING FIREWOOD

If you have an ax and saw available you can produce clean-cut logs from dry firewood, as well as chop kindling.

HOW TO SPLIT LOGS:
Set your log on a block which is at least knee high. Now raise your ax over your head with one hand by your head, the other on the lower end of the handle. As you swing the ax downward the hand by your head slips lower and thus accelerates the entire ax.

ATTENTION:
If the log will not stand up by itself do not hold it with your hands, even when wearing gloves. If you strike next to the log, at best you will only be missing a finger.

When you use an ax your shins are very vulnerable if you miss the block, so the block you use for splitting logs should be wide enough to catch the blow if you miss the log.

F12 HOW TO USE A FIRE PISTON

Next to striking a flint, the "fire piston" was especially popular in Asia, but later also among trappers in the USA.

The advantage of this lighter is that you can use even relatively coarse tinder, like untreated cattail fibers, to start embers → **glowing**. The principle of the fire piston is the same as the diesel engine: auto-ignition by compression.

Put the tinder in the hollow in the piston **(1)**.

This is pushed into the cylinder with force and speed **(2)** and immediately pulled out again. You will see embers **(3)** right away, lit by the over 392°F due to the compressed air.

K 41 FIREARMS

Whether air gun, Airsoft, or a sharp weapon, **always** follow these rules when handling firearms:

>> Never aim any weapon, even unloaded, at any person.

>> If you do not shoot right away, aim the barrel at the ground.

>> Unloaded weapons should be carried with the action open.

>> When shooting, always think about your line of fire and backstop.

Shooting at water, stone, or wood at a shallow angle can cause the bullet to rebound and ricochet.

E30 SEWING YOUR OWN TRAPPER HAT

You can sew yourself a genuine trapper hat from → **tanned hide** in just a few steps. All you need is a knife, a bone piercer, and some → **line**.

Trace a shape somewhat larger than your head circumference on the flesh side of the leather. Draw the following pattern outside it, so you can fold the fur into a cap (fur side is inside). Hold the edges together and prick holes along them, then stitch them together—your winter hat with fold-down ear flaps is finished.

▶ *Using this simple pattern you can sew a warm fur hat with ear flaps.*

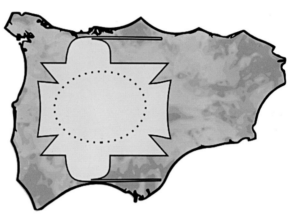

K42 OPEN A CAN WITH YOUR AX

A real trapper does not need an opener to open a can. A good ax can cut sheet metal cans without getting any notches or nicks on the blade.

To make yourself red beans with bacon in the morning when you do not have a can opener, do the following:

STEP 1 Hold the ax head so that the lower cutting edge rests on the can top. Hit the ax with the heel of your hand.

STEP 2 Turn the can about 45° and repeat so that you cut a wedge (make a pointed cut in the can top, not around it).

STEP 3 Bend back the triangle in the can top carefully and you can shake out the contents.

K43 BREW COFFEE LIKE A TRAPPER

After a successful hunt and savoring some whiskey, nothing is more important the next morning than some good, strong coffee. Brewed over the fire and drunk with flat bread baked on the embers, it provides your foundation for a busy day.

All you need is ground coffee and a fireproof cup. First fill the cup with water and add the desired amount of coffee grounds. Now set the cup next to the fire and spread some embers around it with a stick. Let the coffee brew for a good ten minutes. This chars any grounds which get stuck to the edge, giving the coffee a distinctive smoky flavor.

Take the cup off the fire using gloves. Add a slurp of cold water—this makes the coffee grounds sink. Now you can drink as usual—at the end, leave the finger-wide layer of coffee grounds in the cup.

K44 EXPRESS BARBECUE TONGS

You can make barbecue tongs in a few simple steps to stir the embers, carry hot stones, or turn over grilling meat. You need just one branch, forked at the top. Use the powercut to split it, so that it is about eighteen inches long and the fork prongs are no longer than your little finger. Now heat the wood at the center, so that it → **bends** till it forms into "pincers." If the wood gets ragged where you cut it or a bit breaks off, that is no problem. The heat-bending will leave enough wood to hold the pincers together.

TIMBER KNOTS

The timber, or carpenter's knot, is a quick knot used to lift building materials or haul firewood through the forest, but do not use it when your load falling down may cause an accident, nor to secure a person!

STEP 1 Fasten the rope around the fastening point. When pulling back the shorter end, make sure it lies between the long end and the load.

STEP 2 Draw the end piece back so that it forms a loop around the long end of the rope. Now wind the end around itself three to five times.

STEP 3 Pull the knot tight so that the long end will be tightened and the coils of the short end are pushed together. This simple knot immediately binds up under a load and loosens as soon as tension is reduced.

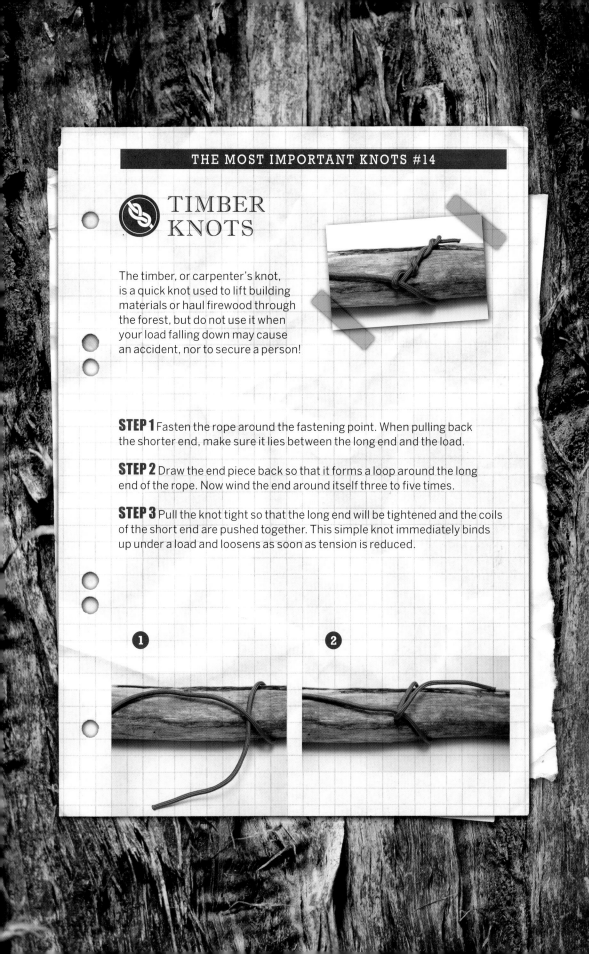

❶

❷

R44 COOKING IN THE DUTCH OVEN

A Dutch oven—in some regions also called a "camp oven"—is a cast iron pot intended for cooking over the fire. In the outdoors it replaces your entire kitchen, since you can use it to roast, boil, and bake.

Before its first use it should be heat-seasoned, because cast iron products are often protected from rust with paraffin or wax. To season, heat the lid and pot on the embers until they stop smoking. Flames may appear in the pot—this does not matter at all. Then reduce heat slightly and cover the pot and lid with grease or oil, which will sputter and smoke.

The pot is now sealed inside by the fat, and nothing will burn or bake onto it. Do not use detergent to wash it, because it might taste of soap.

RECIPE NO. 1: BAKING BREAD

Baking a real loaf of bread outdoors is an art. To do this, prepare a dough from flour and other ingredients like spices, onion, bacon, or dried fruit, and leave the dough to rise.

Meanwhile, place the pot on the fire so that it will be hot. Put some flat stones inside to prevent the dough from touching the pot directly so it will not bake on. Now cover the pot with the top and put a few small embers on top (the cover has a raised edge specifically for this purpose).

After a quarter hour, open the pot and slide in the dough. Cover the pot again and put a very few embers next to the pot—the thick cast iron distributes heat evenly. In about forty-five minutes your bread should be ready.

RECIPE NO. 2: TRAPPER BREAKFAST

A real trapper's breakfast is always good in the morning. You can make fried bacon and eggs on the pot lid.

You do not even need oil for this, since the seasoned cast iron has absorbed enough oil into its pores and bacon contains enough fat. First, arrange the bacon sideways on the edge of the preheated lid. Let it sizzle for a few minutes until some fat collects in the middle. You can break the eggs into this.

Tip: Before serving, tip a shot glass of whiskey or rum into the pan (keep your distance or you could get → **burned**) and flambé your breakfast.

RECIPE NO. 3: VEGETABLE STEW

If you get a taste for vegetable stew outdoors, you can make the best one you have ever eaten with a Dutch oven and a snail shell. How does it work?

First, use a small stone to make a chink in the shell. Now you have a vegetable peeler you can use to scrape the dirty skins from potatoes, carrots, and parsnips. You can also quarter onions, zucchini, celery, leeks, and whatever other vegetables you can get your hands on. For spices, a pinch of salt and some pepper are all you need. After covering the pot, put a piece of coal on top and some more next to the Dutch oven. Keep swapping the coals regularly and let the vegetables cook for about three to four hours. Due to this gentle and uniform cooking at low temperature the vegetables stay crisp and flavorful.

Now the meat version. You can enhance the recipe either right at the start with a leg of badger, pork, or venison, or lay some bacon on top of the vegetables about an hour before the end of cooking.

Peel vegetables elegantly with a snail shell peeler.

K45 BOILING DOWN YOUR MEMENTOS

If you have killed or found a special animal, you might want to preserve the skull as a memento or trophy. You can simply place the skull on an anthill, although then it will often be stolen by a fox or dragged away by birds.

Hunters boil their trophies down and then bleach them. To do this you need a larger pot, a wire, and a knife. You begin by peeling the skin from the head, then cooking the skull in water for up to two hours, depending on the size. It is best do this at an appropriate distance from your cabin—if what you are preparing is no longer fresh, the smell is pretty strong.

If there are antlers or horns on the skull, try to position it so that they do not touch the water. While it boils, you can keep cutting the flesh away from the outside. When well cooked, the remaining strands fall off almost by themselves.

Now bend the wire into a hook and use it to reach into the hole at the base of the skull to loosen the brains and cerebral membranes from the bone. Keep rinsing the entire thing again and again. Before you dry it, you can clean everything again with a brush or a little brushwood and bleach it in a solution of two → **water purification tablets** per quarter gallon water for a few hours.

Flatbread baked on the embers with grilled rate makes a nutritious breakfast.

R45 FLATBREAD ON THE EMBERS

Stickbread is for barbecues with children. Real trappers bake their bread directly on the embers.

Take some flour and mix it with a little water. You can add nuts, onions, leeks, and salt and pepper to taste. Knead the dough either in a pot or on the ground on some foil. The dough should feel firm and not sticky. Now take a handful of dough, shape it into a flat cake, and place it directly on the coals. Don't be shy: Neither embers nor cinders will stick to it, and if you turn it regularly, it also will not burn. After a few moments, take the cake off the fire, press it even thinner, turn it over, and put it back on the fire. Do this every three to five minutes until your cakes are done—and really taste good. The direct heat gives the bread a great taste. They taste best with freshly brewed → **trapper coffee**.

K46 SNAIL LIGHTS

You can make a small, long-burning candle using resin, grease, or fat if you have hunted an animal. It requires a fireproof holder, like a snail shell, and fiber for a wick. First heat the fuel a bit and press it into the holder. Now press a hole down to the bottom of the fuel and leave everything to cool. Thread the wick into the hole and push it all together a bit. Wet the wick with a drop of the fuel. These candles can burn for up to an hour. It is important that the wick is not too long, because otherwise the flame will flare up too much, will smoke, and can possibly ignite the fuel.

K47 SKINNING OFF AN ANIMAL

To skin an animal, cut the fur around the feet in a ring and sever the skin to the "initial cut."

As a rule, the head is cut off and can be → **boiled down**, and the brain is used for → **tanning**. Now "peel" the skin from the legs. If it stays attached, trim if off carefully. This is often the case on the shoulder blades.

Scrape away the fat under the skin; it can be → **melted down**. The cleaned animal should be prepared right away.

NOTE: You can skin small animals like hares, rabbits, or rats before gutting them.

▶

When skinning, you need to be careful so that you do not cut any holes in the skin.

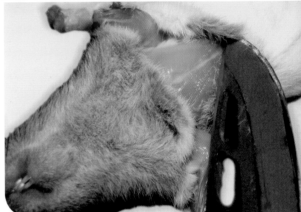

M24 ANTI-HANGOVER DRINK

When you wake up in the morning and your head is buzzing, it may be that you either sat too close to the fire and inhaled smoke, or you were lying in an uncomfortable position all night (such as on an empty bottle). Now you need a tonic and headache remedy. You can make this from the roots and reddish sprouts of the meadowsweet.

Cut the roots of this herb, which grows in almost every roadside ditch, into small pieces and cook out about a tablespoon. It smells strongly like rheumatism ointment, and the roots actually contain salicylates, like those used in headache pills. If you still have a slightly queasy stomach, a teaspoon of white ash (minerals!) in your drink works miracles.

You can recognize meadowsweet by its delicate yellow and intensely sweet-smelling flowers and the taste of the root, which is reminiscent of mouthwash.

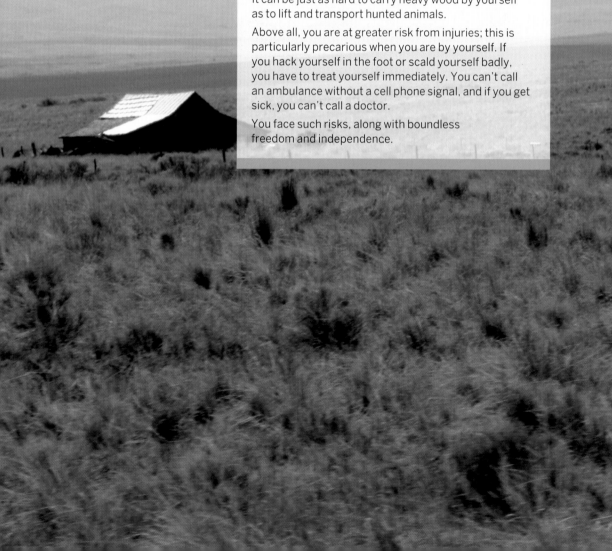

K48 CHOOSING TO BE ALONE

If you live in a remote cabin, you have to contend with problems different from those if you are on the road just a short time.

Not everyone is suited for living alone for a long time. There is no one to comfort, encourage, or praise you. Even everyday tasks are difficult to cope with alone. It can be just as hard to carry heavy wood by yourself as to lift and transport hunted animals.

Above all, you are at greater risk from injuries; this is particularly precarious when you are by yourself. If you hack yourself in the foot or scald yourself badly, you have to treat yourself immediately. You can't call an ambulance without a cell phone signal, and if you get sick, you can't call a doctor.

You face such risks, along with boundless freedom and independence.

K49 TANNING ANIMAL HIDES

Trappers earned their money by selling skins and hides, which they dried and then took to the tanner by canoe. To provide themselves with gloves made of skins or → **fur hats** in winter, trappers often did the tanning in their cabins.

STEP 1 → **Skin off** the fur cleanly; you can cut off the leg pieces. Lay the hide on the fur side and remove everything that is red or white and soft with a flat knife or stone scraper. This is to cut flesh and fat from the rawhide. Make small holes all around the hide for threading a cord.

STEP 2 Now make a stable frame from four branches and stretch the hide tight on it. It shrinks a little as it dries, which is why the cord must be really taut. Put the hide in the shade to dry.

STEP 3 Now light a fire from the thickest possible logs and next to it build a smoker of stones (as shown below) or from wood logs, like for → **smoking meat**.

STEP 4 Lay the hide flesh side down on the smoker. Put the logs—which are charred and smoldering, but no longer burning—in the smoker and replace them regularly. If a log flares up again, take it out quickly and strike it a few times on the ground to put out the flame. Then you can put it back in the smoker. Do not let the air inside get too hot or the skin will cook dry.

After two to three hours, you can again lay the skin out to dry. Then stretch it out and rub it with tallow or the boiled brains. The smoked leather is finished.

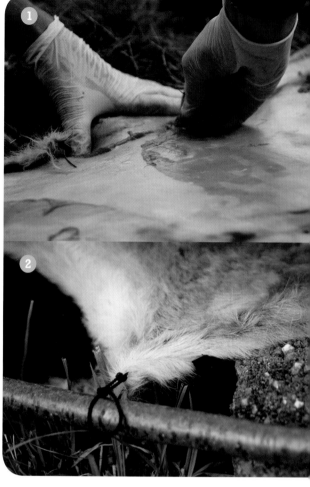

The smoker is made of stones stacked on top of each other to form a "U."

M2.5 HOW TO REPEL MOSQUITOES

A cabin in the shady forest is a small oasis, especially when it is hot. In the rain barrels behind the cabin and in small puddles there is a brood growing that has it in for you: mosquitoes. Besides mosquitoes, a trapper often has to contend with fleas that jump on them when they prepare a skin. You can combat both using plants that can be found on the edge of woods and in clearings:

Tansy is very reliable for scaring away mosquitoes. Simply put the entire plant on the stove, or in the heat of the campfire. The resulting steam scares mosquitoes—if you smoke your clothes or furs in it, even fleas will leave the scene.

M2.6 ASSESSING BURNS

If you often squat by an open fire to work you may burn your hands. This is usually not very dangerous, as long as only small areas are affected. Serious injuries often result from improper handling of highly flammable fuels, or due to carelessness at the campfire.

To estimate how dangerous a burn is you can use the "nine rule." This means dividing the total area of skin into different regions by multiples of nine percent. There are also different degrees of burns:

1ST DEGREE Reddened skin.

2ND DEGREE Blistering.

3RD DEGREE Skin burned black and white.

4TH DEGREE Burn extends under the skin with damage to nerve tissue and muscle.

Injuries above second degree, which affect **about 10% of the body surface**, may be an acute threat to life. The skin damage can cause serious loss of fluid. In this case you should get help as soon as possible.

You can reduce "after-burning"—the burn extending into deeper layers of tissue— to some extent by immediately cooling smaller burns for about half an hour after the accident.

Put a loose, sterile cover on the wounds. Fluid-filled blisters should not be opened because the skin keeps the underlying wounds free of germs. Larger areas of skin may be covered with pieces of a rescue blanket.

Large-scale burns can conceivably have a poor prognosis without intensive care.

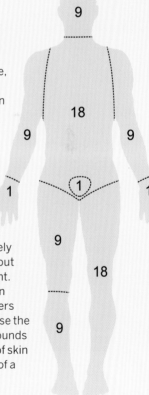

Skin areas for assessing the burn area: From ten percent is life threatening!

R46 BURDOCK: ROOT VEGETABLE

You can recognize burdock safely by the flowers, which are covered with fine, sharp burrs (2). The flowers are often purple or reddish, and recall the shape of small artichokes. The stem, which usually has many branches, is furrowed and has a waxy surface. All parts of the plant are often covered by a hairy felt. The alternating foliage is somewhat heart-shaped and forms an expansive (sometimes ten foot) wreath (1).

Burdock grows huge leaves (3). These can be used for wrapping food when you are collecting it or for baking. They taste so bitter that they are unfit for human consumption in large quantities.

The roots (4) of the burdock, which bears no flowers during its first year, are sometimes as big as sugar beets in autumn. They can be cooked and give you a lot of energy. Sometimes they are a bit woody. In this case, cook them down and only drink the broth.

▲
You can recognize burdock safely by the burrs around the flowers and the large leaves.

K50 OPEN A WINE BOTTLE WITHOUT A CORKSCREW

It is hardly a problem for you to open a beer bottle with a lighter or a folded bill (something you have probably already practiced often). However, wine bottles represent a more serious problem. If, after you have spent a long time in your trapper's cabin, you want to celebrate the final evening with a special wine and do not have a corkscrew, proceed as follows:

Take a solid wire and wind it around the bottle neck directly under the mouth. When it is coiled fast, heat it a bit with a lighter. It will expand and you can wind it around another one or two times. Now let it all cool. The wire creates a predetermined breaking point. With a light tap with an ax from below on the bottle neck, the constricted glass ring breaks off cleanly. The cork can now be pulled easily.

M27 STABLE SIDE POSITION IN FOUR HANDHOLDS

The classic instructions for the so-called "recovery position" sound more like a complicated ground fighting technique from Judo, although the actual goal is simple: The patient should lie in a stable position on their side, with the head tilted and stabilized with the mouth down. **This keeps the airways open and vomit can drain out.**

STEP 1 Turn the victim on their side, so that the chest faces slightly downward, the back slightly upward. When turning the person, you should also take care that neither the shoulder girdle rotates in relation to the hips nor the head tips uncontrollably.

STEP 2 Stabilize the unconscious body around the upper pivot point by pulling or bending the upper leg forward somewhat.

STEP 3 Now carefully stretch the head back slightly and support it with either the patient's palm, or if the arm is injured, with a jacket shaped the same way.

STEP 4 Open the mouth somewhat and check breathing.

When the injured person's body is lying stably on their side, with head tilted and mouth slightly downward, their position is *adequately* stable.

ATTENTION! Never leave an unconscious person lying unattended on their back!

HOW TO COIL A ROPE

Ropes and cords should never be stored untidily in a backpack or boat. Otherwise the lines get tangled, and when you need them fast in a storm or in distress it can take hours to sort them out again. They should always be coiled up properly.

STEP 1 Wind tent lines around four fingers; wind ropes around hand and elbow. It is important that you always coil from the fixed point (tent flap) to the end, or the rope gets twisted.

STEP 2 When you reach the end, unwind two or three coils again. Take the coils from your arm or hand and hold them fast. Wrap the loose end tightly around one end.

STEP 3 Pull the rest of the rope through the resulting opening. Make sure that the end does not slip through the opening. Pull the resulting loop over all the coils. A tug on the end or attachment point secures the coiled rope in a "doll" shape.

❶ ❷ ❸

F13 STRIKING A FIRE WITH CHARCLOTH

Before matches were invented, fires were started with flint and steel. Even today this is still done from tradition.

In fact, striking a fire this way also has a practical value. Blowing on a fire always keeps you fit, and except for the tinder, which you can make yourself outside, striking a fire causes virtually no wear and tear on anything. This method lets you spend the winter in your trapper's cabin without having to worry about running out of fuel for a lighter.

You can make tinder either from old cotton fabric or dry tree fungi, which you stick in a can with a small hole in the lid and set on fire until it smokes vigorously (1). Then plug the hole with a nail and let the can char for half an hour at a lower heat (2). The fire striker consists of a hardened steel striker and flint (Silex), or in an emergency, a knife with a carbon blade and a broken pebble. You can also make a fire striker set with these once you have ignited a flame with a fire saw, for example, and also prepared tinder.

Put the tinder on top of the stone close to a sharp edge. Then use the steel to strike at the stone as precisely and with as rapid a movement as possible (3). Every now and then a spark will land on the tinder. Once this has started to smolder, put it in the → **fire nest** and blow to start the flames.

K51 MAKE YOUR OWN MOUSETRAP

You should generally store food in your trapper's cabin so no animals can get at it. This means storing everything in screw-top jars or cans. If mice dance on the kitchen table during the night (or if they are eating you out of house and home) you can make a universal trap. You can use it to catch mice and rats, as well as small reptiles and birds. It is based on a tube (waste pipe, bamboo, tin can) and a spring-loaded stick, which you attach upright at the closed end of the tube. Now set the trigger—made of two carved hooks turned opposite each other—through a hole in the top. Attach the trap string with a noose with another hook to the trigger, the spring-loaded stick, so that the noose is threaded through a hole near the entry, and the trap will be sprung as soon as an animal slips into the tube and pushes or pulls on the trigger. You can smear some chocolate on the trigger.

◄ *Trap entrance.*

E31 CARVE EATING UTENSILS

If you cook outdoors and have no cutlery with you, you can make your own from soft wood. For a spoon or fork use a similar starting piece: a slightly curved piece of wood. You shape it so that you flatten the bottom surface or tines crosswise and the handle lengthwise.

FORK: If you want to carve a fork, carefully carve away the wood between the outer edges of the lower end until you have two tines. These you can sharpen and harden. To do this, hold the wood close to the embers and let it heat slowly until it is reddish-brown.

SPOON: In contrast to a fork, you carve a spoon by cutting out the upper side either using the → **punch cut** or burn out the bowl by putting embers on the wood. When the spoon bowl and tines are done then work out the shape as you like and smooth it off with sand.

K52 RESIN GLUE

You can make a resin adhesive that bonds well in just a short time. It does not matter whether the resin comes from wounds in pine, fir, or spruce trees, but it must definitely be a conifer. Resin of deciduous trees does not bond well and is therefore unsuitable.

Heat the resin you collected by the fire. You can melt it in a pot or turn it on a bar directly over the coals. When it has melted, mix it with finely grated charcoal in a 1:1 ratio. The resin practically becomes cement, with the charcoal the sand that gives the entirety a certain hardness. Let everything cool. To glue something, heat the resin and use it like a hot-melt adhesive. Immediately after cooling it becomes firm and bonds very well on many natural materials like wood, leather, feathers, and plant fibers.

▲
You should never let the police catch you with this—there is a risk of confusion!

► Heat the wood well directly by the embers at the bending point without letting it char.

K53 HOW TO BEND WOOD

If you need a piece of wood that is particularly straight for a wood frame or need a curved piece to make snowshoes, you can use this method of heat bending to use wood that does not fit.

To bend wood, you just have to heat it properly and then slowly shape it as you want. Since it always springs back some after being bent, bend the wood slightly more than necessary. If the wood is still green and fresh it can be heated directly over the coals.

If it is already completely dry, steam it or smear some clay or mud on the wood before heating. This will keep the wood somewhat damp as it is heated and it will not break.

R47 RENDERING ANIMAL FAT

If you have killed an animal, you should use every part of it you can. The fat is especially valuable because it contains large amounts of energy. You can scrape fat away from under the skin, as well as from the internal organs. Organ fat lies around the kidneys, intestines,

and at the hips. After you have cut out all the white parts, cut the fat into small pieces. If you can, also use the back of your ax to beat it, to break down all the cells. Now take your tallest pot and fill it with water. Place a sieve above the water; you can improvise one using grass or rushes and fasten it with a cord. Put the fat fibers in this sieve. Put the whole thing on the fire and bring it to a boil.

The heat will squeeze the fat from the cells and it will land on the water surface. Since it is heated to 212°F you can eat the pure fat that results, but some medicinal ingredients still remain (for example, in badger or beaver fat).

The carefully rendered fat will keep without refrigeration for some time and will not soon turn rancid. You can now squeeze out what remains in the sieve. After it cools, draw the fat or oil off from the pot and pour it into clean jars.

F 14 SMOKING FOOD ON THE CAMPFIRE

You have probably already frequently grilled food over charcoal. Did you know that grilled food tastes even better when it is cooked over wood?

The trick is selecting the right wood and preparing the fireplace. If you want to give the meat an aromatic, spicy taste, like from a smoker, use dry oak, beech, or hazel. You can make it more acerbic and even smokier with fir or spruce.

To grill something for about an hour, light some logs of the desired wood and let them burn down to coals. If you get enough coals spread them out. Split some more wood as fine as possible and put it in water or pack it in damp soil. Before you set the grate lay this wood sideways on the fireplace. The wood starts to smolder without burning, smokes, and flavors the grilled food— all without expensive wood chips or a smoker.

Is it healthy? Of course not! This is why you have your unadulterated Stone Age taste.

R48 COOKING IN A FIREPIT

If you want to cook larger quantities of meat and vegetables until they are tender as butter, you can prepare them in a fire pit.

STEP 1 To do this, dig a pit in the ground, about one meter deep and wide. Light a fire in it and lay as many large stones on top as possible.

STEP 2 When the fire has burned down to the embers, line the fire pit thickly with large plant leaves, such as →**burdock leaves**. Lay the meat and vegetables on the leaves and then carefully cover this again with leaves.

If you like things particularly tender, then pour some more water into the pit, which immediately seeps in between the stones and hisses as it evaporates.

STEP 3 As quickly as possible, cover everything with earth. Now you need patience. Depending on the amount of vegetables and meat, you wait for between 3 and 6 hours.

Picture at top: Extremely tender, extremely tasty. Here doe venison was seasoned with →fresh balsam seeds and cooked along with →cattails as a vegetable side dish.

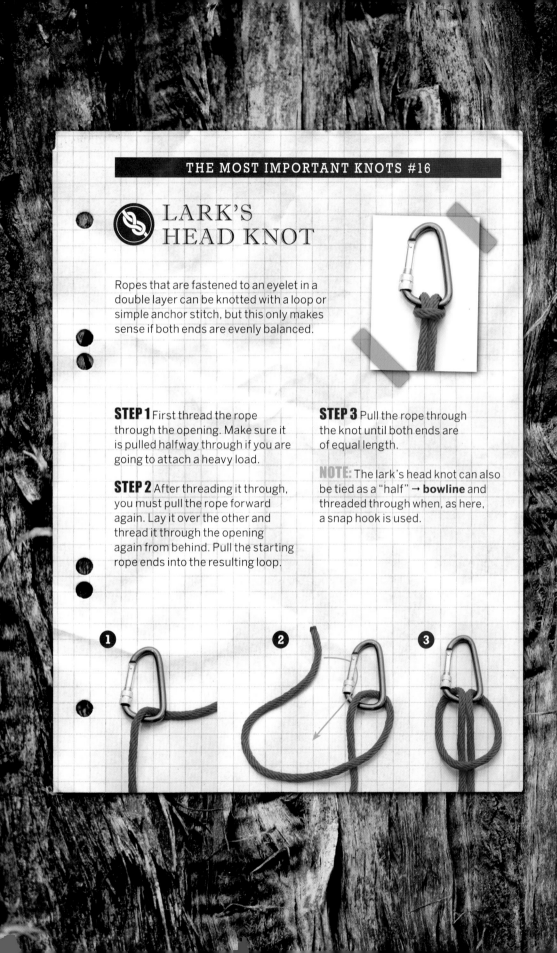

LARK'S HEAD KNOT

Ropes that are fastened to an eyelet in a double layer can be knotted with a loop or simple anchor stitch, but this only makes sense if both ends are evenly balanced.

STEP 1 First thread the rope through the opening. Make sure it is pulled halfway through if you are going to attach a heavy load.

STEP 2 After threading it through, you must pull the rope forward again. Lay it over the other and thread it through the opening again from behind. Pull the starting rope ends into the resulting loop.

STEP 3 Pull the rope through the knot until both ends are of equal length.

NOTE: The lark's head knot can also be tied as a "half" → **bowline** and threaded through when, as here, a snap hook is used.

R49 PEMICAN: NUTRITIOUS ENERGY BOMB

Pemmican can be sliced into bars. Even in freezing temperatures this fat-rich energy bar is easy to chew.
▼

If you are traveling in snow and ice, you need huge amounts of energy to maintain body temperature. You can need so much that you will not get very far on spaghetti and energy bars, especially since the latter will be rock hard at low temperatures and barely edible if not warmed up.

Pemmican is different. It is virtually nothing but pure protein and fat. You can also make it outdoors. Since the whole thing is covered with fat and winter is the usual "pemmican season," this emergency ration keeps for months.

To make it, take the → **rendered fat** from a hunted animal. Another ingredient of pemmican is meat dried by the fire, or if available → **smoked meat**. The meat should be so dry that it can be ground into powder with a pestle. You also need some dried fruit, and preferably some salt and spices. Fill a cup three-quarters full with meat and fruit powder. Fill up the rest with warmed fat. Before it cools fully, press it into a flat cake on a board and cut it into bars.

M28 TREATING CHOPPING INJURIES

If you do not take care when working with an ax or machete serious injury can result. In the worst case you can bleed to death. You must apply a **pressure bandage as soon as possible**. Place the compress from a dressing pack on the wound. Then wind gauze around the limb a couple times, tie a knob (stone, lighter, branch) directly over the wound, and wind around more to increase pressure. If it keeps bleeding add another bandage on top.

If that also does not help, wait a few minutes (as long it does not gush out). Sometimes the clotting blood in the bandage stops further loss. But if the bleeding still does not stop you have to make a tourniquet on yourself, like it or not. Put a strap, paracord, etc., beneath the next joint on the body, stick a branch through it, and turn it until the bleeding is significantly reduced. Only tie a tourniquet this way if you are so far away from help that it might take you a few hours to reach a doctor.

E32 MAKE A HACKSAW

To saw wood into pieces for the night in your trapper's cabin, you can make a simple hacksaw from a saw blade or using a wire or pocket saw from your → **survival kit**. Cut a piece the length of the saw blade from a strong stick of wood and another three pieces about twelve inches long.

On the long piece, cut or saw out oblong tongues (A), which should have the same angle. In two of the shorter pieces, cut two grooves at about the middle using the → **punch cut (B)**, in which the tongues fit exactly. After you stick the pieces together they should hold by themselves. Also cut notches in both ends (on the side facing away from the groove) to hold the saw blade (C) or a paracord. Now fasten the blade to these notches with rings or wire. Press the bars on to the tongues and wind them around with paracord on the other side (→ **clove hitch,** D).

Now take the last of the short pieces, stick it between the cords, and wind it around until the saw blade is held taut (E). Then it is blocked by the long bar.

If you master this technique, you do not have to take all your tools along to your trapper's cabin, but can finish the hacksaw on site.

W21 LAYER WATER FILTER: STATIONARY STERILIZATION

If you stay in one place for a longer time you can construct a large, stationary water filter.

You need a waterproof container, such as a cut plastic bottle or a bark or bamboo tube, with a small hole the size of a needle in the bottom. Then fill it up as follows: At the bottom, put a little wadding, such as from a →**cattail**, (1). Then comes finely pounded coal (2), wadding again (3), and as thick as possible a layer of fine sand (4), wadding (5), fine gravel (6), and wadding (7). At the top, add a slightly coarser mat of fiber (8) to contain algae and leaves. You must put it all together carefully and without shaking it much.

Such a filter can significantly improve water quality, but it is important that **your container is absolutely waterproof**. If you try to use a sock or triangular cloth, as is often described, you might as well forget it—the dirty water will just drip past the filter into your collection vessel.

▲
The various layers in the water filter are separated by fine plant fibers.

K54 SPLITTING WOOD WITHOUT AN AX

There is no alternative to a saw and ax for splitting firewood for the stove in your trapper's cabin, but if you are underway in the woods and want to split a wood sapling to make skis, for example, you won't get very far using a knife or a small hatchet.

You can use the simplest wedge to split the hardest wood. Set the wedge firmly in a natural gap and hammer it in. This will widen the gap a bit, and you can insert the next wedge.

AT THE END

You could read a few sentences here about how to dig a hole when you relieve yourself outdoors, but I assume you have already figured out how to do that. For this reason, I would like to use this quiet outhouse at the end of the book to wish you lots of fun when practicing, and above all broadening, the techniques and skills presented in this book.

Due to the limited number of pages available it is not possible to address and describe fully all conceivable topics.

Nevertheless, I hope this book gives you good enough reason to go outdoors and engage yourself with the infinite variety of survival.

APPENDIX

INDEX BY TOPIC

All topics alphabetically and sorted by the following fields:

FIRE
WATER
SHELTER
RATIONS
MEDICINE
EQUIPMENT
KNOW-HOW/SKILLS
KNOTS
NAVIGATION

RATIONS

MEDICINE

EQUIPMENT

KNOW-HOW/SKILLS

KNOTS

NAVIGATION

ABOUT THE AUTHOR

Johannes "Joe" Vogel is a biologist, author, adventurer, hunter, and fisherman who has written several books on archaic survival (survival with the least possible equipment), gives lectures and seminars throughout Europe, and works for several print magazines, TV channels, and production companies. He is always testing, expanding, and checking his knowledge anew on expeditions and in survival experiments all over the world, and advises individuals on preparing for extreme travel abroad. He acquired the techniques he uses firsthand from original inhabitants, war veterans, and pros in various fields.
You can learn more about Joe and his projects at www.vivalranger.com

Paracord Knife Handle Wraps:
The Complete Guide,
from Tactical to Asian Styles
Jan Dox

This clear, photo-by-photo guide teaches everything you need to know, including selecting appropriate paracord and weaving the correct wrap styles for underlays, tactical uses, skeleton handles, and more. Over 16 styles and approaches are covered, from basic handle wraps to standard military or looped, to paradox, to artistic Japanese tsukamaki wraps.

Size: 6" x 9" | 564 color images | 160 pp
ISBN: 978-0-7643-5425-0 | sprial bound | $24.99

On an Open Fire:
Roasting, Barbecuing, Cooking
Carston Bothe, Editor

Why make a mess in your indoor kitchen when you can build your own fire pit outside? There is something about roasting suckling pig on a spit, duck on a rope, or just chestnuts over a handmade fire pit that makes eating with friends and family more special. Here are a dozen different cooking methods and nearly a hundred recipes.

Size: 7" x 10" | 295 color photos | 168 pp
ISBN: 978-0-7643-4483-1 | soft cover | $29.99

Guide to Knife & Ax Throwing
Dieter Führer

Knife and ax throwing are becoming increasingly popular athletic disciplines. Dieter, a successful competitive pitcher and your personal guide, has tested more than a hundred different throwing objects, and offers plenty of tips from his own experience. Now, you will learn everything you need to know about throwing all forms, from deceptively simple steel throwing knives to hatchets and tomahawks.

Size: 6" x 9" | 119 color photos | 104 pp
ISBN: 978-0-7643-4779-5 | hard cover | $24.99

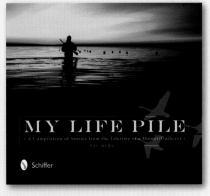

My Life Pile:
A Compilation of Stories from
the Lifetime of a Hunter/Gatherer
Vic Berg

This book tells of the self-centering effects of living within nature while hunting and fishing, written by an outfitter and guide with 50 years experience. The author observes how humbling his clients' dealings with wildlife encountered may be. Learn a lifetime's worth of outfitter's secrets, along with unusual nature facts and proven hunting/fishing strategies.

Size: 9 1/8" x 8 1/8" | 49 color & 4 b/w images | 160 pp
ISBN13: 978-0-7643-4518-0 | soft cover | $19.99

THANKS

For the great cooperation which helped create this book, I want to thank very much: my life partner Patricia Braun —not only for the design and carrying out the concept, but also for her support during all the labor-intensive weeks—as well as Susanne Fischer of Verlag pietsch for her intensive assistance and the highly productive exchange of ideas.

My thanks also go to my "terrain neighbors" in the Karlsruhe-Weingarten and to Waffen-Haffner in Karlsruhe for props.

I furthermore want to thank Laura Lamertz and Alison Paye of Discovery.